ISBN 0-8373-2788-1

C-2788   CAREER EXAMINATION SERIES

This is your PASSBOOK® for...

Librarian I

Test Preparation Study Guide

Questions & Answers

NLC

NATIONAL LEARNING CORPORATION

PASSBOOK®

NOTICE

This book is SOLELY intended for, is sold ONLY to, and its use is RESTRICTED to *individual*, bona fide applicants or candidates who qualify by virtue of having seriously filed applications for appropriate license, certificate, professional and/or promotional advancement, higher school matriculation, scholarship, or other legitimate requirements of educational and/or governmental authorities.

This book is NOT intended for use, class instruction, tutoring, training, duplication, copying, reprinting, excerption, or adaptation, etc., by:

(1) Other publishers

(2) Proprietors and/or Instructors of "Coaching" and/or Preparatory Courses

(3) Personnel and/or Training Divisions of commercial, industrial, and governmental organizations

(4) Schools, colleges, or universities and/or their departments and staffs, including teachers and other personnel

(5) Testing Agencies or Bureaus

(6) Study groups which seek by the purchase of a single volume to copy and/or duplicate and/or adapt this material for use by the group as a whole without having purchased individual volumes for each of the members of the group

(7) Et al.

Such persons would be in violation of appropriate Federal and State statutes.

PROVISION OF LICENSING AGREEMENTS. — Recognized educational commercial, industrial, and governmental institutions and organizations, and others legitimately engaged in educational pursuits, including training, testing, and measurement activities, may address a request for a licensing agreement to the copyright owners, who will determine whether, and under what conditions, including fees and charges, the materials in this book may be used by them. In other words, a licensing facility exists for the legitimate use of the material in this book on other than an individual basis. However, it is asseverated and affirmed here that the material in this book *CANNOT* be used without the receipt of the express permission of such a licensing agreement from the Publishers.

NATIONAL LEARNING CORPORATION
212 Michael Drive
Syosset, New York 11791

Inquiries re licensing agreements should be addressed to:
The President
National Learning Corporation
212 Michael Drive
Syosset, New York 11791

PASSBOOK® SERIES

THE *PASSBOOK® SERIES* has been created to prepare applicants and candidates for the ultimate academic battlefield – the examination room.

At some time in our lives, each and every one of us may be required to take an examination – for validation, matriculation, admission, qualification, registration, certification, or licensure.

Based on the assumption that every applicant or candidate has met the basic formal educational standards, has taken the required number of courses, and read the necessary texts, the *PASSBOOK® SERIES* furnishes the one special preparation which may assure passing with confidence, instead of failing with insecurity. Examination questions – together with answers – are furnished as the basic vehicle for study so that the mysteries of the examination and its compounding difficulties may be eliminated or diminished by a sure method.

This book is meant to help you pass your examination provided that you qualify and are serious in your objective.

The entire field is reviewed through the huge store of content information which is succinctly presented through a provocative and challenging approach – the question-and-answer method.

A climate of success is established by furnishing the correct answers at the end of each test.

You soon learn to recognize types of questions, forms of questions, and patterns of questioning. You may even begin to anticipate expected outcomes.

You perceive that many questions are repeated or adapted so that you can gain acute insights, which may enable you to score many sure points.

You learn how to confront new questions, or types of questions, and to attack them confidently and work out the correct answers.

You note objectives and emphases, and recognize pitfalls and dangers, so that you may make positive educational adjustments.

Moreover, you are kept fully informed in relation to new concepts, methods, practices, and directions in the field.

You discover that you are actually taking the examination all the time: you are preparing for the examination by "taking" an examination, not by reading extraneous and/or supererogatory textbooks.

In short, this PASSBOOK®, used directedly, should be an important factor in helping you to pass your test.

LIBRARIAN I

DUTIES

Performs professional-level librarian duties. Provides advisory and guidance services. Compiles bibliographies, answers reference inquiries, and performs basic cataloging and classification duties. Conducts book talks, multimedia programs, story-and-picture-book hours, and liaison activities with community groups. Supervision may be exercised over nonprofessional staff, and the incumbent may participate in the training of Librarian Trainees. The work is reviewed by a higher-level librarian or administrator through conferences, reports and observation. Does related work as required.

SCOPE OF THE WRITTEN TEST

The written test will cover knowledge, skills, and/or abilities in such areas as:

1. Information technology and the library;
2. Library resources and practices;
3. Librarian/patron relations; and
4. Evaluating conclusions in light of known facts.

HOW TO TAKE A TEST

I. YOU MUST PASS AN EXAMINATION

A. *WHAT EVERY CANDIDATE SHOULD KNOW*

Examination applicants often ask us for help in preparing for the written test. What can I study in advance? What kinds of questions will be asked? How will the test be given? How will the papers be graded?

As an applicant for a civil service examination, you may be wondering about some of these things. Our purpose here is to suggest effective methods of advance study and to describe civil service examinations.

Your chances for success on this examination can be increased if you know how to prepare. Those "pre-examination jitters" can be reduced if you know what to expect. You can even experience an adventure in good citizenship if you know why civil service exams are given.

B. *WHY ARE CIVIL SERVICE EXAMINATIONS GIVEN?*

Civil service examinations are important to you in two ways. As a citizen, you want public jobs filled by employees who know how to do their work. As a job seeker, you want a fair chance to compete for that job on an equal footing with other candidates. The best-known means of accomplishing this two-fold goal is the competitive examination.

Exams are widely publicized throughout the nation. They may be administered for jobs in federal, state, city, municipal, town or village governments or agencies.

Any citizen may apply, with some limitations, such as the age or residence of applicants. Your experience and education may be reviewed to see whether you meet the requirements for the particular examination. When these requirements exist, they are reasonable and applied consistently to all applicants. Thus, a competitive examination may cause you some uneasiness now, but it is your privilege and safeguard.

C. *HOW ARE CIVIL SERVICE EXAMS DEVELOPED?*

Examinations are carefully written by trained technicians who are specialists in the field known as "psychological measurement," in consultation with recognized authorities in the field of work that the test will cover. These experts recommend the subject matter areas or skills to be tested; only those knowledges or skills important to your success on the job are included. The most reliable books and source materials available are used as references. Together, the experts and technicians judge the difficulty level of the questions.

Test technicians know how to phrase questions so that the problem is clearly stated. Their ethics do not permit "trick" or "catch" questions. Questions may have been tried out on sample groups, or subjected to statistical analysis, to determine their usefulness.

Written tests are often used in combination with performance tests, ratings of training and experience, and oral interviews. All of these measures combine to form the best-known means of finding the right person for the right job.

II. HOW TO PASS THE WRITTEN TEST

A. NATURE OF THE EXAMINATION

To prepare intelligently for civil service examinations, you should know how they differ from school examinations you have taken. In school you were assigned certain definite pages to read or subjects to cover. The examination questions were quite detailed and usually emphasized memory. Civil service exams, on the other hand, try to discover your present ability to perform the duties of a position, plus your potentiality to learn these duties. In other words, a civil service exam attempts to predict how successful you will be. Questions cover such a broad area that they cannot be as minute and detailed as school exam questions.

In the public service similar kinds of work, or positions, are grouped together in one "class." This process is known as *position-classification*. All the positions in a class are paid according to the salary range for that class. One class title covers all of these positions, and they are all tested by the same examination.

B. FOUR BASIC STEPS

1) Study the announcement

How, then, can you know what subjects to study? Our best answer is: "Learn as much as possible about the class of positions for which you've applied." The exam will test the knowledge, skills and abilities needed to do the work.

Your most valuable source of information about the position you want is the official exam announcement. This announcement lists the training and experience qualifications. Check these standards and apply only if you come reasonably close to meeting them.

The brief description of the position in the examination announcement offers some clues to the subjects which will be tested. Think about the job itself. Review the duties in your mind. Can you perform them, or are there some in which you are rusty? Fill in the blank spots in your preparation.

Many jurisdictions preview the written test in the exam announcement by including a section called "Knowledge and Abilities Required," "Scope of the Examination," or some similar heading. Here you will find out specifically what fields will be tested.

2) Review your own background

Once you learn in general what the position is all about, and what you need to know to do the work, ask yourself which subjects you already know fairly well and which need improvement. You may wonder whether to concentrate on improving your strong areas or on building some background in your fields of weakness. When the announcement has specified "some knowledge" or "considerable knowledge," or has used adjectives like "beginning principles of…" or "advanced … methods," you can get a clue as to the number and difficulty of questions to be asked in any given field. More questions, and hence broader coverage, would be included for those subjects which are more important in the work. Now weigh your strengths and weaknesses against the job requirements and prepare accordingly.

3) Determine the level of the position

Another way to tell how intensively you should prepare is to understand the level of the job for which you are applying. Is it the entering level? In other words, is this the position in which beginners in a field of work are hired? Or is it an intermediate or advanced level? Sometimes this is indicated by such words as "Junior" or "Senior" in the class title. Other jurisdictions use Roman numerals to designate the level – Clerk I, Clerk II, for example. The word "Supervisor" sometimes appears in the title. If the level is not indicated by the title, check the description of duties. Will you be working under very close supervision, or will you have responsibility for independent decisions in this work?

4) Choose appropriate study materials

Now that you know the subjects to be examined and the relative amount of each subject to be covered, you can choose suitable study materials. For beginning level jobs, or even advanced ones, if you have a pronounced weakness in some aspect of your training, read a modern, standard textbook in that field. Be sure it is up to date and has general coverage. Such books are normally available at your library, and the librarian will be glad to help you locate one. For entry-level positions, questions of appropriate difficulty are chosen – neither highly advanced questions, nor those too simple. Such questions require careful thought but not advanced training.

If the position for which you are applying is technical or advanced, you will read more advanced, specialized material. If you are already familiar with the basic principles of your field, elementary textbooks would waste your time. Concentrate on advanced textbooks and technical periodicals. Think through the concepts and review difficult problems in your field.

These are all general sources. You can get more ideas on your own initiative, following these leads. For example, training manuals and publications of the government agency which employs workers in your field can be useful, particularly for technical and professional positions. A letter or visit to the government department involved may result in more specific study suggestions, and certainly will provide you with a more definite idea of the exact nature of the position you are seeking.

III. KINDS OF TESTS

Tests are used for purposes other than measuring knowledge and ability to perform specified duties. For some positions, it is equally important to test ability to make adjustments to new situations or to profit from training. In others, basic mental abilities not dependent on information are essential. Questions which test these things may not appear as pertinent to the duties of the position as those which test for knowledge and information. Yet they are often highly important parts of a fair examination. For very general questions, it is almost impossible to help you direct your study efforts. What we can do is to point out some of the more common of these general abilities needed in public service positions and describe some typical questions.

1) General information

Broad, general information has been found useful for predicting job success in some kinds of work. This is tested in a variety of ways, from vocabulary lists to questions about current events. Basic background in some field of work, such as sociology or economics, may be sampled in a group of questions. Often these are principles which have become familiar to most persons through exposure rather than through formal training. It is difficult to advise you how to study for these questions; being alert to the world around you is our best suggestion.

2) Verbal ability

An example of an ability needed in many positions is verbal or language ability. Verbal ability is, in brief, the ability to use and understand words. Vocabulary and grammar tests are typical measures of this ability. Reading comprehension or paragraph interpretation questions are common in many kinds of civil service tests. You are given a paragraph of written material and asked to find its central meaning.

3) Numerical ability

Number skills can be tested by the familiar arithmetic problem, by checking paired lists of numbers to see which are alike and which are different, or by interpreting charts and graphs. In the latter test, a graph may be printed in the test booklet which you are asked to use as the basis for answering questions.

4) Observation

A popular test for law-enforcement positions is the observation test. A picture is shown to you for several minutes, then taken away. Questions about the picture test your ability to observe both details and larger elements.

5) Following directions

In many positions in the public service, the employee must be able to carry out written instructions dependably and accurately. You may be given a chart with several columns, each column listing a variety of information. The questions require you to carry out directions involving the information given in the chart.

6) Skills and aptitudes

Performance tests effectively measure some manual skills and aptitudes. When the skill is one in which you are trained, such as typing or shorthand, you can practice. These tests are often very much like those given in business school or high school courses. For many of the other skills and aptitudes, however, no short-time preparation can be made. Skills and abilities natural to you or that you have developed throughout your lifetime are being tested.

Many of the general questions just described provide all the data needed to answer the questions and ask you to use your reasoning ability to find the answers. Your best preparation for these tests, as well as for tests of facts and ideas, is to be at your physical and mental best. You, no doubt, have your own methods of getting into an exam-taking mood and keeping "in shape." The next section lists some ideas on this subject.

IV. KINDS OF QUESTIONS

Only rarely is the "essay" question, which you answer in narrative form, used in civil service tests. Civil service tests are usually of the short-answer type. Full instructions for answering these questions will be given to you at the examination. But in case this is your first experience with short-answer questions and separate answer sheets, here is what you need to know:

1) Multiple-choice Questions

Most popular of the short-answer questions is the "multiple choice" or "best answer" question. It can be used, for example, to test for factual knowledge, ability to solve problems or judgment in meeting situations found at work.

A multiple-choice question is normally one of three types—
- It can begin with an incomplete statement followed by several possible endings. You are to find the one ending which *best* completes the statement, although some of the others may not be entirely wrong.
- It can also be a complete statement in the form of a question which is answered by choosing one of the statements listed.

- It can be in the form of a problem – again you select the best answer.

Here is an example of a multiple-choice question with a discussion which should give you some clues as to the method for choosing the right answer:

When an employee has a complaint about his assignment, the action which will *best* help him overcome his difficulty is to
  A. discuss his difficulty with his coworkers
  B. take the problem to the head of the organization
  C. take the problem to the person who gave him the assignment
  D. say nothing to anyone about his complaint

In answering this question, you should study each of the choices to find which is best. Consider choice "A" – Certainly an employee may discuss his complaint with fellow employees, but no change or improvement can result, and the complaint remains unresolved. Choice "B" is a poor choice since the head of the organization probably does not know what assignment you have been given, and taking your problem to him is known as "going over the head" of the supervisor. The supervisor, or person who made the assignment, is the person who can clarify it or correct any injustice. Choice "C" is, therefore, correct. To say nothing, as in choice "D," is unwise. Supervisors have and interest in knowing the problems employees are facing, and the employee is seeking a solution to his problem.

2) True/False Questions

The "true/false" or "right/wrong" form of question is sometimes used. Here a complete statement is given. Your job is to decide whether the statement is right or wrong.

SAMPLE: A roaming cell-phone call to a nearby city costs less than a non-roaming call to a distant city.

This statement is wrong, or false, since roaming calls are more expensive.

This is not a complete list of all possible question forms, although most of the others are variations of these common types. You will always get complete directions for answering questions. Be sure you understand *how* to mark your answers – ask questions until you do.

V. RECORDING YOUR ANSWERS

Computer terminals are used more and more today for many different kinds of exams.

For an examination with very few applicants, you may be told to record your answers in the test booklet itself. Separate answer sheets are much more common. If this separate answer sheet is to be scored by machine – and this is often the case – it is highly important that you mark your answers correctly in order to get credit.

An electronic scoring machine is often used in civil service offices because of the speed with which papers can be scored. Machine-scored answer sheets must be marked with a pencil, which will be given to you. This pencil has a high graphite content which responds to the electronic scoring machine. As a matter of fact, stray dots may register as answers, so do not let your pencil rest on the answer sheet while you are pondering the correct answer. Also, if your pencil lead breaks or is otherwise defective, ask for another.

Since the answer sheet will be dropped in a slot in the scoring machine, be careful not to bend the corners or get the paper crumpled.

The answer sheet normally has five vertical columns of numbers, with 30 numbers to a column. These numbers correspond to the question numbers in your test booklet. After each number, going across the page are four or five pairs of dotted lines. These short dotted lines have small letters or numbers above them. The first two pairs may also have a "T" or "F" above the letters. This indicates that the first two pairs only are to be used if the questions are of the true-false type. If the questions are multiple choice, disregard the "T" and "F" and pay attention only to the small letters or numbers.

Answer your questions in the manner of the sample that follows:

32. The largest city in the United States is
    A. Washington, D.C.
    B. New York City
    C. Chicago
    D. Detroit
    E. San Francisco

1) Choose the answer you think is best. (New York City is the largest, so "B" is correct.)
2) Find the row of dotted lines numbered the same as the question you are answering. (Find row number 32)
3) Find the pair of dotted lines corresponding to the answer. (Find the pair of lines under the mark "B.")
4) Make a solid black mark between the dotted lines.

VI. BEFORE THE TEST

Common sense will help you find procedures to follow to get ready for an examination. Too many of us, however, overlook these sensible measures. Indeed, nervousness and fatigue have been found to be the most serious reasons why applicants fail to do their best on civil service tests. Here is a list of reminders:

- Begin your preparation early – Don't wait until the last minute to go scurrying around for books and materials or to find out what the position is all about.
- Prepare continuously – An hour a night for a week is better than an all-night cram session. This has been definitely established. What is more, a night a week for a month will return better dividends than crowding your study into a shorter period of time.
- Locate the place of the exam – You have been sent a notice telling you when and where to report for the examination. If the location is in a different town or otherwise unfamiliar to you, it would be well to inquire the best route and learn something about the building.
- Relax the night before the test – Allow your mind to rest. Do not study at all that night. Plan some mild recreation or diversion; then go to bed early and get a good night's sleep.
- Get up early enough to make a leisurely trip to the place for the test – This way unforeseen events, traffic snarls, unfamiliar buildings, etc. will not upset you.
- Dress comfortably – A written test is not a fashion show. You will be known by number and not by name, so wear something comfortable.

- Leave excess paraphernalia at home – Shopping bags and odd bundles will get in your way. You need bring only the items mentioned in the official notice you received; usually everything you need is provided. Do not bring reference books to the exam. They will only confuse those last minutes and be taken away from you when in the test room.
- Arrive somewhat ahead of time – If because of transportation schedules you must get there very early, bring a newspaper or magazine to take your mind off yourself while waiting.
- Locate the examination room – When you have found the proper room, you will be directed to the seat or part of the room where you will sit. Sometimes you are given a sheet of instructions to read while you are waiting. Do not fill out any forms until you are told to do so; just read them and be prepared.
- Relax and prepare to listen to the instructions
- If you have any physical problem that may keep you from doing your best, be sure to tell the test administrator. If you are sick or in poor health, you really cannot do your best on the exam. You can come back and take the test some other time.

VII. AT THE TEST

The day of the test is here and you have the test booklet in your hand. The temptation to get going is very strong. Caution! There is more to success than knowing the right answers. You must know how to identify your papers and understand variations in the type of short-answer question used in this particular examination. Follow these suggestions for maximum results from your efforts:

1) Cooperate with the monitor

The test administrator has a duty to create a situation in which you can be as much at ease as possible. He will give instructions, tell you when to begin, check to see that you are marking your answer sheet correctly, and so on. He is not there to guard you, although he will see that your competitors do not take unfair advantage. He wants to help you do your best.

2) Listen to all instructions

Don't jump the gun! Wait until you understand all directions. In most civil service tests you get more time than you need to answer the questions. So don't be in a hurry. Read each word of instructions until you clearly understand the meaning. Study the examples, listen to all announcements and follow directions. Ask questions if you do not understand what to do.

3) Identify your papers

Civil service exams are usually identified by number only. You will be assigned a number; you must not put your name on your test papers. Be sure to copy your number correctly. Since more than one exam may be given, copy your exact examination title.

4) Plan your time

Unless you are told that a test is a "speed" or "rate of work" test, speed itself is usually not important. Time enough to answer all the questions will be provided, but this does not mean that you have all day. An overall time limit has been set. Divide the total time (in minutes) by the number of questions to determine the approximate time you have for each question.

5) Do not linger over difficult questions

If you come across a difficult question, mark it with a paper clip (useful to have along) and come back to it when you have been through the booklet. One caution if you do this – be sure to skip a number on your answer sheet as well. Check often to be sure that you have not lost your place and that you are marking in the row numbered the same as the question you are answering.

6) Read the questions

Be sure you know what the question asks! Many capable people are unsuccessful because they failed to *read* the questions correctly.

7) Answer all questions

Unless you have been instructed that a penalty will be deducted for incorrect answers, it is better to guess than to omit a question.

8) Speed tests

It is often better NOT to guess on speed tests. It has been found that on timed tests people are tempted to spend the last few seconds before time is called in marking answers at random – without even reading them – in the hope of picking up a few extra points. To discourage this practice, the instructions may warn you that your score will be "corrected" for guessing. That is, a penalty will be applied. The incorrect answers will be deducted from the correct ones, or some other penalty formula will be used.

9) Review your answers

If you finish before time is called, go back to the questions you guessed or omitted to give them further thought. Review other answers if you have time.

10) Return your test materials

If you are ready to leave before others have finished or time is called, take ALL your materials to the monitor and leave quietly. Never take any test material with you. The monitor can discover whose papers are not complete, and taking a test booklet may be grounds for disqualification.

VIII. EXAMINATION TECHNIQUES

1) Read the general instructions carefully. These are usually printed on the first page of the exam booklet. As a rule, these instructions refer to the timing of the examination; the fact that you should not start work until the signal and must stop work at a signal, etc. If there are any *special* instructions, such as a choice of questions to be answered, make sure that you note this instruction carefully.

2) When you are ready to start work on the examination, that is as soon as the signal has been given, read the instructions to each question booklet, underline any key words or phrases, such as *least, best, outline, describe* and the like. In this way you will tend to answer as requested rather than discover on reviewing your paper that you *listed without describing*, that you selected the *worst* choice rather than the *best* choice, etc.

3) If the examination is of the objective or multiple-choice type – that is, each question will also give a series of possible answers: A, B, C or D, and you are called upon to select the best answer and write the letter next to that answer on your answer paper – it is advisable to start answering each question in turn. There may be anywhere from 50 to 100 such questions in the three or four hours allotted and you can see how much time would be taken if you read through all the questions before beginning to answer any. Furthermore, if you come across a question or group of questions which you know would be difficult to answer, it would undoubtedly affect your handling of all the other questions.

4) If the examination is of the essay type and contains but a few questions, it is a moot point as to whether you should read all the questions before starting to answer any one. Of course, if you are given a choice – say five out of seven and the like – then it is essential to read all the questions so you can eliminate the two that are most difficult. If, however, you are asked to answer all the questions, there may be danger in trying to answer the easiest one first because you may find that you will spend too much time on it. The best technique is to answer the first question, then proceed to the second, etc.

5) Time your answers. Before the exam begins, write down the time it started, then add the time allowed for the examination and write down the time it must be completed, then divide the time available somewhat as follows:
   • If 3-1/2 hours are allowed, that would be 210 minutes. If you have 80 objective-type questions, that would be an average of 2-1/2 minutes per question. Allow yourself no more than 2 minutes per question, or a total of 160 minutes, which will permit about 50 minutes to review.
   • If for the time allotment of 210 minutes there are 7 essay questions to answer, that would average about 30 minutes a question. Give yourself only 25 minutes per question so that you have about 35 minutes to review.

6) The most important instruction is to *read each question* and make sure you know what is wanted. The second most important instruction is to *time yourself properly* so that you answer every question. The third most important instruction is to *answer every question*. Guess if you have to but include something for each question. Remember that you will receive no credit for a blank and will probably receive some credit if you write something in answer to an essay question. If you guess a letter – say "B" for a multiple-choice question – you may have guessed right. If you leave a blank as an answer to a multiple-choice question, the examiners may respect your feelings but it will not add a point to your score. Some exams may penalize you for wrong answers, so in such cases *only*, you may not want to guess unless you have some basis for your answer.

7) Suggestions
   a. Objective-type questions
      1. Examine the question booklet for proper sequence of pages and questions
      2. Read all instructions carefully
      3. Skip any question which seems too difficult; return to it after all other questions have been answered
      4. Apportion your time properly; do not spend too much time on any single question or group of questions

5. Note and underline key words – *all, most, fewest, least, best, worst, same, opposite,* etc.
6. Pay particular attention to negatives
7. Note unusual option, e.g., unduly long, short, complex, different or similar in content to the body of the question
8. Observe the use of "hedging" words – *probably, may, most likely,* etc.
9. Make sure that your answer is put next to the same number as the question
10. Do not second-guess unless you have good reason to believe the second answer is definitely more correct
11. Cross out original answer if you decide another answer is more accurate; do not erase until you are ready to hand your paper in
12. Answer all questions; guess unless instructed otherwise
13. Leave time for review

b. Essay questions
1. Read each question carefully
2. Determine exactly what is wanted. Underline key words or phrases.
3. Decide on outline or paragraph answer
4. Include many different points and elements unless asked to develop any one or two points or elements
5. Show impartiality by giving pros and cons unless directed to select one side only
6. Make and write down any assumptions you find necessary to answer the questions
7. Watch your English, grammar, punctuation and choice of words
8. Time your answers; don't crowd material

8) Answering the essay question

Most essay questions can be answered by framing the specific response around several key words or ideas. Here are a few such key words or ideas:

M's: manpower, materials, methods, money, management
P's: purpose, program, policy, plan, procedure, practice, problems, pitfalls, personnel, public relations
a. Six basic steps in handling problems:
1. Preliminary plan and background development
2. Collect information, data and facts
3. Analyze and interpret information, data and facts
4. Analyze and develop solutions as well as make recommendations
5. Prepare report and sell recommendations
6. Install recommendations and follow up effectiveness

b. Pitfalls to avoid
1. *Taking things for granted* – A statement of the situation does not necessarily imply that each of the elements is necessarily true; for example, a complaint may be invalid and biased so that all that can be taken for granted is that a complaint has been registered

2. *Considering only one side of a situation* – Wherever possible, indicate several alternatives and then point out the reasons you selected the best one
3. *Failing to indicate follow up* – Whenever your answer indicates action on your part, make certain that you will take proper follow-up action to see how successful your recommendations, procedures or actions turn out to be
4. *Taking too long in answering any single question* – Remember to time your answers properly

IX. AFTER THE TEST

Scoring procedures differ in detail among civil service jurisdictions although the general principles are the same. Whether the papers are hand-scored or graded by machine we have described, they are nearly always graded by number. That is, the person who marks the paper knows only the number – never the name – of the applicant. Not until all the papers have been graded will they be matched with names. If other tests, such as training and experience or oral interview ratings have been given, scores will be combined. Different parts of the examination usually have different weights. For example, the written test might count 60 percent of the final grade, and a rating of training and experience 40 percent. In many jurisdictions, veterans will have a certain number of points added to their grades.

After the final grade has been determined, the names are placed in grade order and an eligible list is established. There are various methods for resolving ties between those who get the same final grade – probably the most common is to place first the name of the person whose application was received first. Job offers are made from the eligible list in the order the names appear on it. You will be notified of your grade and your rank as soon as all these computations have been made. This will be done as rapidly as possible.

People who are found to meet the requirements in the announcement are called "eligibles." Their names are put on a list of eligible candidates. An eligible's chances of getting a job depend on how high he stands on this list and how fast agencies are filling jobs from the list.

When a job is to be filled from a list of eligibles, the agency asks for the names of people on the list of eligibles for that job. When the civil service commission receives this request, it sends to the agency the names of the three people highest on this list. Or, if the job to be filled has specialized requirements, the office sends the agency the names of the top three persons who meet these requirements from the general list.

The appointing officer makes a choice from among the three people whose names were sent to him. If the selected person accepts the appointment, the names of the others are put back on the list to be considered for future openings.

That is the rule in hiring from all kinds of eligible lists, whether they are for typist, carpenter, chemist, or something else. For every vacancy, the appointing officer has his choice of any one of the top three eligibles on the list. This explains why the person whose name is on top of the list sometimes does not get an appointment when some of the persons lower on the list do. If the appointing officer chooses the second or third eligible, the No. 1 eligible does not get a job at once, but stays on the list until he is appointed or the list is terminated.

X. HOW TO PASS THE INTERVIEW TEST

The examination for which you applied requires an oral interview test. You have already taken the written test and you are now being called for the interview test – the final part of the formal examination.

You may think that it is not possible to prepare for an interview test and that there are no procedures to follow during an interview. Our purpose is to point out some things you can do in advance that will help you and some good rules to follow and pitfalls to avoid while you are being interviewed.

What is an interview supposed to test?

The written examination is designed to test the technical knowledge and competence of the candidate; the oral is designed to evaluate intangible qualities, not readily measured otherwise, and to establish a list showing the relative fitness of each candidate – as measured against his competitors – for the position sought. Scoring is not on the basis of "right" and "wrong," but on a sliding scale of values ranging from "not passable" to "outstanding." As a matter of fact, it is possible to achieve a relatively low score without a single "incorrect" answer because of evident weakness in the qualities being measured.

Occasionally, an examination may consist entirely of an oral test – either an individual or a group oral. In such cases, information is sought concerning the technical knowledges and abilities of the candidate, since there has been no written examination for this purpose. More commonly, however, an oral test is used to supplement a written examination.

Who conducts interviews?

The composition of oral boards varies among different jurisdictions. In nearly all, a representative of the personnel department serves as chairman. One of the members of the board may be a representative of the department in which the candidate would work. In some cases, "outside experts" are used, and, frequently, a businessman or some other representative of the general public is asked to serve. Labor and management or other special groups may be represented. The aim is to secure the services of experts in the appropriate field.

However the board is composed, it is a good idea (and not at all improper or unethical) to ascertain in advance of the interview who the members are and what groups they represent. When you are introduced to them, you will have some idea of their backgrounds and interests, and at least you will not stutter and stammer over their names.

What should be done before the interview?

While knowledge about the board members is useful and takes some of the surprise element out of the interview, there is other preparation which is more substantive. It *is* possible to prepare for an oral interview – in several ways:

1) Keep a copy of your application and review it carefully before the interview

This may be the only document before the oral board, and the starting point of the interview. Know what education and experience you have listed there, and the sequence and dates of all of it. Sometimes the board will ask you to review the highlights of your experience for them; you should not have to hem and haw doing it.

2) Study the class specification and the examination announcement

Usually, the oral board has one or both of these to guide them. The qualities, characteristics or knowledges required by the position sought are stated in these documents. They offer valuable clues as to the nature of the oral interview. For example, if the job involves supervisory responsibilities, the announcement will usually indicate that knowledge of modern supervisory methods and the qualifications of the candidate as a supervisor will be tested. If so, you can expect such questions, frequently in the form of a hypothetical situation which you are expected to solve. NEVER go into an oral without knowledge of the duties and responsibilities of the job you seek.

3) Think through each qualification required

Try to visualize the kind of questions you would ask if you were a board member. How well could you answer them? Try especially to appraise your own knowledge and background in each area, *measured against the job sought*, and identify any areas in which you are weak. Be critical and realistic – do not flatter yourself.

4) Do some general reading in areas in which you feel you may be weak

For example, if the job involves supervision and your past experience has NOT, some general reading in supervisory methods and practices, particularly in the field of human relations, might be useful. Do NOT study agency procedures or detailed manuals. The oral board will be testing your understanding and capacity, not your memory.

5) Get a good night's sleep and watch your general health and mental attitude

You will want a clear head at the interview. Take care of a cold or any other minor ailment, and of course, no hangovers.

What should be done on the day of the interview?

Now comes the day of the interview itself. Give yourself plenty of time to get there. Plan to arrive somewhat ahead of the scheduled time, particularly if your appointment is in the fore part of the day. If a previous candidate fails to appear, the board might be ready for you a bit early. By early afternoon an oral board is almost invariably behind schedule if there are many candidates, and you may have to wait. Take along a book or magazine to read, or your application to review, but leave any extraneous material in the waiting room when you go in for your interview. In any event, relax and compose yourself.

The matter of dress is important. The board is forming impressions about you – from your experience, your manners, your attitude, and your appearance. Give your personal appearance careful attention. Dress your best, but not your flashiest. Choose conservative, appropriate clothing, and be sure it is immaculate. This is a business interview, and your appearance should indicate that you regard it as such. Besides, being well groomed and properly dressed will help boost your confidence.

Sooner or later, someone will call your name and escort you into the interview room. *This is it.* From here on you are on your own. It is too late for any more preparation. But remember, you asked for this opportunity to prove your fitness, and you are here because your request was granted.

What happens when you go in?

The usual sequence of events will be as follows: The clerk (who is often the board stenographer) will introduce you to the chairman of the oral board, who will introduce you to the other members of the board. Acknowledge the introductions before you sit down. Do not be surprised if you find a microphone facing you or a stenotypist sitting by. Oral interviews are usually recorded in the event of an appeal or other review.

Usually the chairman of the board will open the interview by reviewing the highlights of your education and work experience from your application – primarily for the benefit of the other members of the board, as well as to get the material into the record. Do not interrupt or comment unless there is an error or significant misinterpretation; if that is the case, do not hesitate. But do not quibble about insignificant matters. Also, he will usually ask you some question about your education, experience or your present job – partly to get you to start talking and to establish the interviewing "rapport." He may start the actual questioning, or turn it over to one of the other members. Frequently, each member undertakes the questioning on a particular area, one in which he is perhaps most competent, so you can expect each member to participate in the examination. Because time is limited, you may also expect some rather abrupt switches in the direction the questioning takes, so do not be upset by it. Normally, a board member will not pursue a single line of questioning unless he discovers a particular strength or weakness.

After each member has participated, the chairman will usually ask whether any member has any further questions, then will ask you if you have anything you wish to add. Unless you are expecting this question, it may floor you. Worse, it may start you off on an extended, extemporaneous speech. The board is not usually seeking more information. The question is principally to offer you a last opportunity to present further qualifications or to indicate that you have nothing to add. So, if you feel that a significant qualification or characteristic has been overlooked, it is proper to point it out in a sentence or so. Do not compliment the board on the thoroughness of their examination – they have been sketchy, and you know it. If you wish, merely say, "No thank you, I have nothing further to add." This is a point where you can "talk yourself out" of a good impression or fail to present an important bit of information. Remember, *you close the interview yourself.*

The chairman will then say, "That is all, Mr. _____, thank you." Do not be startled; the interview is over, and quicker than you think. Thank him, gather your belongings and take your leave. Save your sigh of relief for the other side of the door.

How to put your best foot forward

Throughout this entire process, you may feel that the board individually and collectively is trying to pierce your defenses, seek out your hidden weaknesses and embarrass and confuse you. Actually, this is not true. They are obliged to make an appraisal of your qualifications for the job you are seeking, and they want to see you in your best light. Remember, they must interview all candidates and a non-cooperative candidate may become a failure in spite of their best efforts to bring out his qualifications. Here are 15 suggestions that will help you:

1) Be natural – Keep your attitude confident, not cocky

If you are not confident that you can do the job, do not expect the board to be. Do not apologize for your weaknesses, try to bring out your strong points. The board is interested in a positive, not negative, presentation. Cockiness will antagonize any board member and make him wonder if you are covering up a weakness by a false show of strength.

2) Get comfortable, but don't lounge or sprawl

Sit erectly but not stiffly. A careless posture may lead the board to conclude that you are careless in other things, or at least that you are not impressed by the importance of the occasion. Either conclusion is natural, even if incorrect. Do not fuss with your clothing, a pencil or an ashtray. Your hands may occasionally be useful to emphasize a point; do not let them become a point of distraction.

3) Do not wisecrack or make small talk

This is a serious situation, and your attitude should show that you consider it as such. Further, the time of the board is limited – they do not want to waste it, and neither should you.

4) Do not exaggerate your experience or abilities

In the first place, from information in the application or other interviews and sources, the board may know more about you than you think. Secondly, you probably will not get away with it. An experienced board is rather adept at spotting such a situation, so do not take the chance.

5) If you know a board member, do not make a point of it, yet do not hide it

Certainly you are not fooling him, and probably not the other members of the board. Do not try to take advantage of your acquaintanceship – it will probably do you little good.

6) Do not dominate the interview

Let the board do that. They will give you the clues – do not assume that you have to do all the talking. Realize that the board has a number of questions to ask you, and do not try to take up all the interview time by showing off your extensive knowledge of the answer to the first one.

7) Be attentive

You only have 20 minutes or so, and you should keep your attention at its sharpest throughout. When a member is addressing a problem or question to you, give him your undivided attention. Address your reply principally to him, but do not exclude the other board members.

8) Do not interrupt

A board member may be stating a problem for you to analyze. He will ask you a question when the time comes. Let him state the problem, and wait for the question.

9) Make sure you understand the question

Do not try to answer until you are sure what the question is. If it is not clear, restate it in your own words or ask the board member to clarify it for you. However, do not haggle about minor elements.

10) Reply promptly but not hastily

A common entry on oral board rating sheets is "candidate responded readily," or "candidate hesitated in replies." Respond as promptly and quickly as you can, but do not jump to a hasty, ill-considered answer.

11) Do not be peremptory in your answers

A brief answer is proper – but do not fire your answer back. That is a losing game from your point of view. The board member can probably ask questions much faster than you can answer them.

12) Do not try to create the answer you think the board member wants

He is interested in what kind of mind you have and how it works – not in playing games. Furthermore, he can usually spot this practice and will actually grade you down on it.

13) Do not switch sides in your reply merely to agree with a board member

Frequently, a member will take a contrary position merely to draw you out and to see if you are willing and able to defend your point of view. Do not start a debate, yet do not surrender a good position. If a position is worth taking, it is worth defending.

14) Do not be afraid to admit an error in judgment if you are shown to be wrong

The board knows that you are forced to reply without any opportunity for careful consideration. Your answer may be demonstrably wrong. If so, admit it and get on with the interview.

15) Do not dwell at length on your present job .

The opening question may relate to your present assignment. Answer the question but do not go into an extended discussion. You are being examined for a *new* job, not your present one. As a matter of fact, try to phrase ALL your answers in terms of the job for which you are being examined.

Basis of Rating

Probably you will forget most of these "do's" and "don'ts" when you walk into the oral interview room. Even remembering them all will not ensure you a passing grade. Perhaps you did not have the qualifications in the first place. But remembering them will help you to put your best foot forward, without treading on the toes of the board members.

Rumor and popular opinion to the contrary notwithstanding, an oral board wants you to make the best appearance possible. They know you are under pressure – but they also want to see how you respond to it as a guide to what your reaction would be under the pressures of the job you seek. They will be influenced by the degree of poise you display, the personal traits you show and the manner in which you respond.

ABOUT THIS BOOK

This book contains tests divided into Examination Sections. Go through each test, answering every question in the margin. We have also attached a sample answer sheet at the back of the book that can be removed and used. At the end of each test look at the answer key and check your answers. On the ones you got wrong, look at the right answer choice and learn. Do not fill in the answers first. Do not memorize the questions and answers, but understand the answer and principles involved. On your test, the questions will likely be different from the samples. Questions are changed and new ones added. If you understand these past questions you should have success with any changes that arise. Tests may consist of several types of questions. We have additional books on each subject should more study be advisable or necessary for you. Finally, the more you study, the better prepared you will be. This book is intended to be the last thing you study before you walk into the examination room. Prior study of relevant texts is also recommended. NLC publishes some of these in our Fundamental Series. Knowledge and good sense are important factors in passing your exam. Good luck also helps. So now study this Passbook, absorb the material contained within and take that knowledge into the examination. Then do your best to pass that exam.

———

EXAMINATION SECTION

EXAMINATION SECTION
TEST 1

DIRECTIONS: Each question or incomplete statement is followed by several suggested answers or completions. Select the one that BEST answers the question or completes the statement. *PRINT THE LETTER OF THE CORRECT ANSWER IN THE SPACE AT THE RIGHT.*

1. For the librarian in charge of preserving information, digital imaging technology has several advantages. Which of the following is NOT one of these?   1._____

    A. Duplication without degradation
    B. Ease of manipulation
    C. Stable and settled technology
    D. Preview capability

2. In contrast to filtering software, a proxy server can be used to   2._____
    I. eliminate access to a set list of Internet sites
    II. limit the access of public workstations to certain electronic resources
    III. eliminate Web-based e-mail
    IV. build a firewall

    A. I and II
    B. I, II and III
    C. II and III
    D. I, II, III and IV

3. In data that is prepared in the cataloging-in-publication (CIP) format and distributed in MARC format prior to a work's publication, the FIRST element to be listed, under the "main entry" heading, is usually the   3._____

    A. uniform title
    B. first named author on the title page
    C. title
    D. statement of responsibility

4. In the United States, most public and academic libraries that depend on public funding use a fiscal year beginning on   4._____

    A. January 15
    B. April 1
    C. July 1
    D. October 1

5. The advantages to entering into a consortial license for print and electronic resources typically include each of the following, EXCEPT   5._____

    A. low-cost access to title of lesser interest
    B. guaranteed control over price increases
    C. level playing field for researchers in the consortium, regardless of institutional affiliation
    D. discounts for libraries that choose electronic-only subscriptions

6. Disadvantages associated with online information searches include   6.__
   - I. scarcity of reputable sources
   - II. slow results delivery
   - III. false hits from items that contain keywords but don't match the topic
   - IV. overwhelming numbers of results

   A. I and II
   B. I, II and III
   C. III and IV
   D. I, II, III and IV

7. The _____ fields in the MARC system contain series statements.   7.__

   A. 0XX
   B. 2XX
   C. 4XX
   D. 6XX

8. Which of the following is a searchable directory of more than a thousand companies that   8.__
   sell library products, and which can be browsed by products and services?

   A. *Librarian's Datebook*
   B. *CNET*
   C. *Library Automation Resources*
   D. *Librarians Online Warehouse*

9. Public service functions of a library staff include each of the following, EXCEPT   9.__

   A. circulation
   B. cataloging
   C. interlibrary loan/document delivery
   D. online services

10. A library professional is about to post to a news group made up of other professionals.   10.__
    Before posting, he may be about to commit a breach of etiquette if he

    A. deselects the HTML option
    B. lurks
    C. presses *Caps Lock*
    D. intends to use several emoticons

11. MIME is an electronic metadata standard that is used to describe files according to   11.__

    A. data type
    B. digital object
    C. object model relationships between digital objects and their subparts

12. Tying together intranet-, Internet-, and vendor-based resources from a single point of   12.__
    access is a function that is performed by _____ software.

    A. database
    B. meta-search
    C. browser
    D. directory

13. For a digital object to maintain its integrity, a user must be able to locate it definitively and reliably among other objects over time. This feature of information integrity is known as   13.____

    A. provenance
    B. fixity
    C. reference
    D. context

14. A one-to-many asynchronous tool that lets many users read and post messages is a(n)   14.____

    A. newsgroup
    B. bulletin board system
    C. chat room
    D. online conference

15. The ideal relative humidity (RH) for permanent storage of library and archival materials is about _____ percent.   15.____

    A. 20-25
    B. 40-45
    C. 60-65
    D. 80-85

16. Which of the following is NOT a service offered by Blackwell?   16.____

    A. Collection development assistance
    B. Approval management
    C. Acquisition services
    D. Online bibliographic and full-text database

17. The DOI system serves to identify and exchange intellectual property on the Internet. The "D" in DOI stands for   17.____

    A. document
    B. domain
    C. digital
    D. decimal

18. The _____ governs the application of new headings to items as they are added to the collection.   18.____

    A. master list
    B. uniform resource locator
    C. authority file
    D. Reader's Guide

19. Most print indexes   19.____
    I. are published annually
    II. help users see how a subject fits into a field of knowledge by using subheadings and cross-references
    III. involve a greater likelihood than electronic indexes of finding something that, while not initially sought, proves valuable
    IV. include the full text of the articles in the index

    A. I only   B. I and II   C. I, II and III   D. I, II, III and IV

20. What is the term for a customizable Internet gateway to a subject-oriented community or package of resources?

    A. Plug-in
    B. Hot link
    C. Portal
    D. Acrobat

20.

21. What is another term for the level of descriptive detail in a record created to represent a document or information resource for the purpose of retrieval?

    A. Granularity
    B. Complexity
    C. Ponderance
    D. Padding

21.

22. A librarian in the process of removing all but one occurrence of a bibliographic record from a file of machine-readable records is said to be

    A. deduping
    B. stringing
    C. weeding
    D. winnowing

22.

23. Of the following, a bibliography is LEAST likely to be found

    A. in an appendix
    B. at the end of an article
    C. at the end of an abstract
    D. at the end of a section

23.

24. Which of the following electronic databases is provided at no cost to libraries?

    A. Ingenta
    B. EBSCO
    C. Catchword
    D. Row-Com's Information Quest (IQ)

24.

25. The Library Services and Technology Act of 1996 distributes federal funds to state library agencies under a formula based on

    A. existing staffing levels
    B. population
    C. the size of existing holdings
    D. documented financial need

25.

KEY (CORRECT ANSWERS)

1.	C		11.	A
2.	C		12.	B
3.	B		13.	C
4.	C		14.	D
5.	D		15.	B
6.	C		16.	D
7.	C		17.	C
8.	D		18.	C
9.	B		19.	C
10.	C		20.	C

21.	A
22.	A
23.	C
24.	C
25.	B

———

TEST 2

DIRECTIONS: Each question or incomplete statement is followed by several suggested answers or completions. Select the one that BEST answers the question or completes the statement. *PRINT THE LETTER OF THE CORRECT ANSWER IN THE SPACE AT THE RIGHT.*

1. The module of the library automation system that is used to modify MARC records is the   1._

     A. acquisitions module
     B. cataloging module
     C. OPAC
     D. circulation module

2. In networking, bandwidth refers to the   2._

     A. data handling capacity of a network or node
     B. amount of data that can be carried by the media in a fixed amount of time
     C. protocols used for Internet information
     D. speed at which a modem or line operates

3. As a general rule, reference materials in an academic library   3._

     A. may be used anywhere in the library
     B. are kept on reserve
     C. are not listed in the catalog
     D. do not circulate

4. Which is NOT typically an element of serials control at a library?   4._

     A. Invoice processing
     B. Binding
     C. Bibliographic database maintenance
     D. Receiving

5. Which of the following enables users to recreate paper documents into searchable, view-able electronic files?   5._

     A. PDF
     B. OCR
     C. HTML
     D. XML

6. Before a library signs a license agreement with an online journal database vendor, it will need to decide if receiving usage statistics is important. The guidelines for statistical measures of usage developed by the International Coalition of Library Consortia (ICOLC) recommends the inclusion of the number of _____ in the criteria for measuring the usage of full-text resources.   6._

     I. queries
     II. "turn-aways"
     III. menu selections counts
     IV. items examined (viewed, bookmarked, downloaded, printed, e-mailed, etc.)

A.   I only
B.   I and III
C.   II, III and IV
D.   I, II, III and IV

7.   Advantages associated with using the Web to set up an electronic reserves (ER) system usually include each of the following, EXCEPT

7.____

A.   no time limits
B.   unlimited copies
C.   more streamlined copyright issues
D.   anytime, anywhere access

8.   In a licensing contract with an electronic journal publisher or packager, each of the following is MOST likely to appear in the attachments, EXCEPT

8.____

A.   assignment clause
B.   payment options
C.   the license period
D.   a clear statement of the price

9.   The Online Computer Library Center (OCLC) has established a set of input standards for entering bibliographic data into its online union catalog. Data the cataloger must enter to meet the designated standard for a specific encoding level is denoted

9.____

A.   M
B.   R
C.   X
D.   C

10.   In using digital imaging technology to store information, the minimum resolution required for maintaining fidelity to an original document is usually considered to be _____ dots per inch (dpi).

10.____

A.   100
B.   300
C.   600
D.   900

11.   Which of the following is LEAST likely to be used as a measure of peak use for a library system?

11.____

A.   Workstations per average number of patrons present
B.   Transaction log
C.   Gate count
D.   Circulation statistics

12.   The most significant problem still facing libraries who make use of multimedia technology is the

12.____

A.   high degree of sophistication required to make use of new technologies
B.   lack of interoperability between proprietary applications and hardware
C.   complexity of the contract law involved in negotiating a site license
D.   amount of data storage consumed by sound and full-motion video

13. Which of the following is considered a "user-centered" method for evaluating a library collection?   13.__

    A. Satisfaction surveys
    B. Age of materials
    C. Items per user
    D. Rate of growth/items added per year

14. In online bibliographic databases, descriptors appear in the _____ field of the record.   14.__

    A. author
    B. subject
    C. keyword
    D. title

15. Compared to a standard workstation, a server tends to have   15.__
    I. network software installed
    II. more RAM
    III. a faster processor
    IV. fewer direct attachments to peripherals

    A. I and II
    B. II and III
    C. III only
    D. I, II, III and IV

16. Subsidiary rights   16.__
    I. include foreign publication
    II. include control over commercial exploitation and reproduction not covered under fair use
    III. are not subject to formal agreement to author and publisher
    IV. cannot be sold or transferred by the person or entity that holds them

    A. I and II
    B. I, II and III
    C. II only
    D. I, II, III and IV

17. One of the major disadvantages associated with screen-reading software used at library workstations is that it   17.__

    A. is useful only for those who know Braille
    B. recites in a mechanical, unnatural-sounding voice
    C. is only available to patrons who can use a standard mouse and keyboard
    D. does not recognize images

18. Which measure of library use is computed by dividing circulation by number of items owned?   18.__

    A. Circulation threshold
    B. Turnaround
    C. Reversion
    D. Turnover

19. Which of the following is NOT a difficulty involved in cataloging or indexing information so that users can easily locate it?   19.____

    A. Existing protocols and standards for cataloging and indexing are too variable, and too vague, to give librarians enough direction.
    B. Interpreting an author's meaning or intent is sometimes difficult.
    C. The different ways in which multiple users might search for information are hard to anticipate.
    D. Cataloging and indexing is a subjective process that allows for ambiguity.

20. The Colon Classification system developed by S.R. Ranganathan is an example of a(n) _____ classification system.   20.____

    A. synthetic
    B. enumerative
    C. decimal
    D. hierarchical

21. Traditionally, the library function of _____ delivery has always been outsourced to a certain extent.   21.____

    A. technical processing
    B. cataloging
    C. acquisitions
    D. document delivery

22. According to the *Anglo-American Cataloging Rules (AACR2)*, if _____ or fewer persons or bodies are primarily responsible for a work, the main entry is under the heading for the first-named author. Other works are described as having "diffuse authorship."   22.____

    A. 2
    B. 3
    C. 4
    D. 5

23. The *Statistical Abstract of the United States* is an example of a(n)   23.____

    A. atlas
    B. bibliography
    C. yearbook
    D. abstract

24. The Principles for Licensing Electronic Resources developed by the ALA, SLA, and others include   24.____
    I. A license agreement should hold the licensee responsible for unauthorized uses of the licensed resource by its users.
    II. The licensor is responsible for establishing policies that create an environment in which authorized users make appropriate use of licensed resources and for carrying out due process when it appears that a use may violate the agreement.

III. The terms of a license should be considered fixed at the time the license is signed by both parties.

IV. A license agreement should require the use of an authentication system that may be a barrier to access by authorized users under particular circumstances.

A. I and II
B. II, III and IV
C. III only
D. I, II, III and IV

25. One way to expand searches in Web-based directories or search engines is to perform truncation, which locates words with variations in spelling or endings. In most Web search engines, the _____ symbol is used after the word for this purpose.   25._

A. asterisk (*)
B. pound (#)
C. plus (+)
D. question mark (?)

———

KEY (CORRECT ANSWERS)

1.	B		11.	A
2.	B		12.	D
3.	D		13.	A
4.	C		14.	B
5.	A		15.	B
6.	D		16.	A
7.	C		17.	D
8.	A		18.	D
9.	A		19.	A
10.	B		20.	A

21.	D
22.	B
23.	C
24.	C
25.	A

———

EXAMINATION SECTION
TEST 1

DIRECTIONS: Each question or incomplete statement is followed by several suggested answers or completions. Select the one that BEST answers the question or completes the statement. *PRINT THE LETTER OF THE CORRECT ANSWER IN THE SPACE AT THE RIGHT.*

1. Electronic library catalogs and periodical indexes differ from Web search engines in each of the following ways, EXCEPT that   1.____

    A. they put cataloged and indexed information through an editorial and publishing process
    B. they contain information that is cataloged and indexed by computers
    C. they can be searched by subject headings that are assigned by the indexer
    D. they include only information that has been selected by an indexer

2. The contents of a typical reference book are about _____ than the book's copyright date   2.____

    A. a year newer
    B. a year older
    C. two years older
    D. three years older

3. An acceptable use policy   3.____

    A. identifies access-blocking rules for filtering software
    B. explains First Amendment protections of freedom of speech in the library
    C. defines a curriculum for teaching users ethical and responsible computer use
    D. states the rules that govern computer, network and/or Internet use and the consequences of violations

4. Which of the following would NOT be a reason for a library staff's decision to develop an expert system?   4.____

    A. There is high staff turnover
    B. The problem is repetitive and expensive.
    C. Human experts are widely available.
    D. The problem is complex.

5. Elements of a library security plan, organized by a library security officer, typically include   5.____
    I. acceptable use policy/policies for online resources
    II. a survey of the library's collections
    III. standard operating procedures for dealing with theft
    IV. a review of the physical layout

    A. I and II
    B. I and III
    C. II, III and IV
    D. I, II, III and IV

6. Some library systems contain auxiliary systems programs that are initiated at startup and executed in the background to perform a task when needed-for example, checking incoming e-mail messages for addresses that cannot be found. These programs are known as

    A. bots
    B. crawlers
    C. macros
    D. daemons

6._

7. The programming interface that enables a Web browser to be an interface to information services other than Web sites is a(n)

    A. DOI
    B. CGI
    C. OPAC
    D. GUI

7._

8. HTML is most appropriate for delivering

    A. business-to-business e-commerce
    B. documents that originated from paper
    C. dynamic data
    D. static information

8._

9. The semantic relationship between the words "bibliography" and "heading" is

    A. generic
    B. passive
    C. associative
    D. partitive

9._

10. The Online Computer Library Center (OCLC) has established a set of input standards for entering bibliographic data into its online union catalog. Data generated by the cataloging system that cannot be altered by the cataloger is denoted

    A. R
    B. SS
    C. X
    D. O

10._

11. What is the term for the form of the book as it is used today?

    A. Incipit
    B. Folio
    C. Index
    D. Codex

11._

12. In indexing, a parenthetical qualifier is likely to be used for each of the following, EXCEPT to

    A. distinguish homographs
    B. give the context of an obscure word or phrase

12._

C. indicate the intended use or meaning of the term in the indexing language
D. specify the academic discipline in which a subject is studied

13. The common measurement of the internal speed of a computer's processor is   13.____

 A. megahertz (MHz)
 B. bits per second (bps)
 C. kilobytes per second (Kbps)
 D. gigabytes (GB)

14. In _____ classification, each subject is developed to the point of indivisibility and a nota-   14.____
tion assigned for every subdivision

 A. hierarchical
 B. enumerative
 C. synthetic
 D. dichotomous

15. In Walford's *Guide to Reference Material,* religion is included in the same volume as   15.____

 A. literature
 B. social sciences
 C. humanities
 D. generalia

16. A group of librarians is meeting to determine the selection of electronic journals for a   16.____
library's collection. One of the MOST likely disadvantages of including the existing electronic resources coordinator in this group is that she may not

 A. have the expertise for many of the subjects
 B. understand the issues or technology involved
 C. have the motivation or commitment
 D. be in a position to develop access interfaces

17. Which of the following is NOT a general review publication?   17.____

 A. *Quill & Quire*
 B. *CHOICE*
 C. *Lambda Book Report*
 D. *Booklist*

18. In networking, a cable is plugged into the _____ of each workstation on the network.   18.____

 A. NIC
 B. GUI
 C. LAN
 D. twisted pair

19. The PDF format is MOST typically used to transmit and store   19.____

 A. static data
 B. business-to-business e-commerce documents
 C. visually rich content
 D. database output

20. The turnover rate for media items in a library is usually measured in   20._

    A. hours
    B. days
    C. weeks
    D. months

21. Which of the following is considered the basis of a "collection-centered" method for eval-   21._
uating a library collection?

    A. Percent of relative use (PRU)
    B. In-house use studies
    C. Comparison to recommended lists
    D. Interlibrary loan statistics

22. In a MARC record for an electronic journal database, the _____ field contains the URL   22._
to the database, but not to any specific journal title.

    A. 538
    B. 710
    C. 856
    D. 949 .

23. Which of the following is a device used to scan and audibly read the information printed   23._
on a written page?

    A. Screen-reading software
    B. OCR software
    C. Kurzweil Reader
    D. TTY

24. A regional public library has ordered a packaged electronic journals database. The ven-   24._
dor asks for the "class" of the library's network. The systems librarian doesn't quite know
how to answer this. She knows that the network accommodates 256 IP addresses. This
network would be considered a class

    A. A
    B. B
    C. C
    D. D

25. From the library's point of view, a license agreement with an electronic journal publisher   25._
or packager should
    I.   indemnify the publisher against third-party claims
    II.   permit access to users who are off-site
    III.   provide for archiving of content if publication or service ceases
    IV.   define hardware, browser, and networking requirements

    A. I and II
    B. I and IV
    C. II, III and IV
    D. I, II, III and IV

KEY (CORRECT ANSWERS)

1.	B		11.	D
2.	B		12.	C
3.	D		13.	A
4.	C		14.	B
5.	C		15.	B
6.	D		16.	A
7.	B		17.	C
8.	D		18.	A
9.	D		19.	C
10.	B		20.	B

21.	C
22.	C
23.	C
24.	C
25.	C

———

TEST 2

DIRECTIONS: Each question or incomplete statement is followed by several suggested answers or completions. Select the one that BEST answers the question or completes the statement. *PRINT THE LETTER OF THE CORRECT ANSWER IN THE SPACE AT THE RIGHT.*

1. The Digital Millenium Copyright Act of 1998 provides for each of the following, EXCEPT a(n)

    A. prohibition against circumventing technological measures used to protect copy-righted works
    B. limitation of liability for online service providers
    C. prohibition against altering information imbedded in digital works by copyright own-ers
    D. extension of the term of copyright to the author's lifetime plus 70 years

    1 _____

2. In the URL *http://www.sparkslib.org:80/index.html,* the *80* is a reference to a

    A. parameter
    B. file
    C. port
    D. protocol

    2 _____

3. Which of the following assistive technologies offers patrons who have difficulty hearing a means of communicating with library staff members?

    A. Touchpad or trackball controller
    B. TTY
    C. On-screen keyboard
    D. Screen-reading software

    3 _____

4. A user wants access to SEC filings of public companies on the Internet, including pro-spectuses, annual reports, 10K reports, and 10Q reports. The user should be directed to

    A. www.sec.gov
    B. the Thomas Register
    C. Lexis/Nexis
    D. EDGAR

    4 _____

5. Which of the following is a term for a software program that searches intelligently for information on the World Wide Web?

    A. Daemon
    B. Pathfinder
    C. Crawler
    D. Sorter

    5 _____

6. In a MARC record for an electronic journal that is separately cataloged, the complement to the 530 note is the linking entry field for a link to another format. This is the _____ field.

    A. 538   B. 776   C. 856   D. 949

    6 _____

7. What is the term for a complete revision of a Dewey Decimal class?   7._____

    A. Reconstruction
    B. Phoenix
    C. Rebridgement
    D. Overhaul

8. Which of the following network topologies tends to be faster and involve the least amount   8._____
    of cabling?

    A. Ring
    B. Matrix
    C. Bus
    D. Star

9. The method of choice for most libraries in authenticating access to electronic journals   9._____
    databases is

    A. User ID
    B. IP address
    C. Password
    D. User ID and password

10. Which of the following is one of S.R. Ranganathan's Five Laws of Library Science?   10._____

    A. The pen is mightier than the sword.
    B. Save the time of the reader.
    C. Every reader knows the book he/she wants to read already; it's just a matter of
        finding it.
    D. Information longs to be free.

11. The semantic relationship between the words "chapbook" and "pamphlet" is   11._____

    A. hierarchic
    B. locative
    C. associative
    D. synonymous

12. Which of the following is NOT a leading vendor of library management software?   12._____

    A. Logos
    B. Endeavor
    C. Auto-Graphics
    D. Sirsi

13. A systems librarian discovers old magnetic tapes in storage, which came from an obso-   13._____
    lete computer system. The only way to read the data in the new library system is to write
    a special program. This method of bringing old data into new systems is referred to as
    data

    A. copying   B. conversion
    C. reformatting   D. migration

14. Which of the following is LEAST likely to be categorized as a social science?   14

     A. History
     B. Law
     C. Journalism
     D. Anthropology

15. What is the term for a classified display in a thesaurus of indexing terms that shows the   15
complete hierarchy of descriptors, from the broadest to the most specific, usually by
indention?

     A. Tree structure
     B. Indexing matrix
     C. Dichotomous key
     D. Cant

16. Which of the following storage media has the greatest storage capacity?   16

     A. ZIP disk
     B. CD-RW
     C. CD-ROM
     D. DVD-ROM

17. A _____ license with an electronic database publisher is a unilateral license who terms   17
are accepted with the software package is opened.

     A. shrink-wrap
     B. force majeure
     C. click-wrap
     D. pay-per-view

18. One way to limit search results in Web search engines and directories is to use phrase   18
searching, which involves

     A. using Boolean terms such as AND or NOT
     B. putting quotation marks around the search words
     C. putting parentheses around the search words
     D. putting an asterisk after the search words

19. In book sales, the largest discounts offered by publishers are typically _____ discounts.   19

     A. trade
     B. cash
     C. library
     D. convention

20. Reference software is NOT the most appropriate learning tool when users want to   20

     A. investigate topics that may be beyond their reading capabilities
     B. browse a number of topics
     C. learn how to perform a specific task
     D. ask a specific question

21. The holdings of all the libraries in a library system, in which libraries owning at least one copy of an item are identified by name and/or location symbol, are always accessible from the

    A. union catalog
    B. bibliographic database
    C. OPAC
    D. reference desk

21.____

22. An overview article on a particular topic is MOST likely to be found in a(n)

    A. encyclopedia
    B. index
    C. gazetteer
    D. dictionary

22.____

23. In the MARC record, the same digits are assigned across fields in the second and third character positions of the tag to indicate data of the same type. For example, tags reading "X51" contain information about

    A. personal names
    B. topical terms
    C. bibliographic titles
    D. geographic names

23.____

24. Generally, XML is NOT

    A. capable of storing context as well as content
    B. considered to be the optimal format for file compression and delivery
    C. able to display dynamic information as a document
    D. an excellent standard for business-to-business applications such as invoices and purchase orders

24.____

25. The USA Patriot Act provides that law enforcement agencies can compel libraries to
    I.   produce circulation records
    II. provide Internet usage records
    III. remain silent about the existence of any warrants served on the library
    IV. reveal patron registration information

    A. I and II
    B. I, II and III
    C. II and III
    D. I, II, III and IV

25.____

KEY (CORRECT ANSWERS)

1.	D		11.	D
2.	C		12.	A
3.	B		13.	D
4.	D		14.	C
5.	C		15.	A
6.	B		16.	D
7.	B		17.	A
8.	C		18.	B
9.	B		19.	A
10.	B		20.	C

21.	A
22.	A
23.	D
24.	B
25.	D

———

EXAMINATION SECTION
TEST 1

DIRECTIONS: Each question or incomplete statement is followed by several suggested answers or completions. Select the one that BEST answers the question or completes the statement. *PRINT THE LETTER OF THE CORRECT ANSWER IN THE SPACE AT THE RIGHT.*

1. The heart of a MARC record for a separately-cataloged electronic journal is contained in the _____ fields

    A. 0XX
    B. 3XX
    C. 5XX
    D. 7XX

    1.____

2. Which of the following is NOT an online acquisitions tool?

    A. *JSTOR*
    B. *Blackwell's Collection Manager*
    C. *Books in Print*
    D. *GOBI*

    2.____

3. The in-house approach to digital imaging and preservation typically offers each of the following advantages, EXCEPT

    A. heightened security
    B. learning by doing
    C. quality assurance
    D. predictable per-image costs

    3.____

4. The publication date of a reference book is usually found on the

    A. back cover
    B. title page
    C. page immediately before the title page
    D. page immediately following the title page

    4.____

5. In the Dublin Core Metadata Initiative, an international effort to develop standard mechanisms for searching online resources, the "type" element provides information about the

    A. topic of the content of the resource, typically expressed as keywords or classification codes
    B. rights held in and over the resource
    C. nature or genre of the content of the resource
    D. extent or scope of the resource's content

    5.____

6. _____ indexing is a method in which the subject headings or descriptors assigned to document s represent simple concepts that the user must combine at the time of searching to retrieve information on a complex subject.

    A. String   B. Assignment
    C. Pre-coordinate   D. Post-coordinate

    6.____

7. A library server would most likely NOT be used as   7.

    A. a terminal for searching online resources such as periodical databases
    B. a file server hosting work processing and other office software, along with staff documents and other files
    C. the host computer for the library's automation system
    D. a connection point between the library and the Internet

8. Under copyright law, any rights that eventually revert to the copyright holder when the   8.
time period or purpose stated in the contract has elapsed or been discharged are known
as _____ rights.

    A. volume
    B. serial
    C. residual
    D. subsidiary

9. Research indicates that to most library professionals, _____ is the most frequently   9.
applied criterion for evaluating the appropriateness of bibliographic references.

    A. quality
    B. topicality
    C. novelty
    D. availability

10. The best way to minimize the substrate deformation and mistracking of magnetic media   10.
is to

    A. use acetate, rather than polyester
    B. limit playback as much as possible
    C. store the media in constant temperature and humidity
    D. store the media in a room that is warmer and more humid than the rest of the library

11. Which of the following is NOT an advantage associated with purchasing an electronic   11.
journal collection in the form of a commercially packaged product?

    A. Good way to track usage
    B. Searchability of articles from other publishers
    C. Lower price per title
    D. Single search interface

12. In the Dewey Decimal Classification System, works in Natural Sciences and Mathematics   12.
are classified in the number category

    A. 000
    B. 300
    C. 500
    D. 700

13. A library's OPAC allows users to turn off images in Web pages and see only the text during searches. This is an example of interface management called   13.____

    A. ghosting
    B. graceful degradation
    C. funneling
    D. cache emptying

14. Which of the following events in library automation occurred FIRST?   14.____

    A. The growing importance of "add-ons" related to the delivery of digital content
    B. Integration into the Web environment
    C. The development of the machine-readable catalog record (MARC)
    D. Integration of library systems with learning management systems

15. One of the main advantages associated with searching for information using print indexes is that they   15.____

    A. provide cross-references to other topics
    B. are usually faster than online searches
    C. tend to yield information that is more accurate
    D. are usually more current

16. Which of the following statements about online link resolvers is FALSE?   16.____

    A. They are applications designed to match source citations with target resources.
    B. Most do not store data, but merely establish links.
    C. Most accept citation information in the form of an OpenURL.
    D. They are designed to take into account which materials a user is authorized by subscription or licensing agreement to access.

17. The intended purpose of copyright law is NOT to   17.____

    A. deter others from plagiarizing a work
    B. ensure a fair return on an author's or publisher's investment of time and money into the creation of a work
    C. provide an author or publisher with the incentive to produce a work by granting a limited monopoly
    D. reward innovators at the expense of consumers

18. When using a library's OPAC, a patron moves the mouse to pass a cursor over an image in the Web page and holds the cursor over the image for several seconds. A text message pops up, replacing the information content of the image. This feature, designed for visually impaired users, is enabled by the use of _____ in coding the page.   18.____

    A. applets
    B. alt tags
    C. plug-ins
    D. SGML

19. A search of a database containing 100 records relevant to a topic retrieves 50 records, 25 of which are relevant to the topic. The search is said to have a _____ percent recall.

   A. 10
   B. 25
   C. 50
   D. 75

20. In a bibliography compiled in the MLA format, the authorship of a book by Tom and Bridget Jones would be indicated

   A. Jones, Tom and Bridget Jones
   B. Jones, Tom and Bridget
   C. Jones, Tom and Jones, Bridget
   D. Tom Jones and Bridget Jones

21. In most large libraries, the _____ record is attached to the bibliographic record for a serial title or multivolume item to track issues, parts, or volumes as they are acquired by the library.

   A. item
   B. check-in
   C. order
   D. holdings

22. Which of the following is an online bibliographic database vendor that charges on a per-search basis?

   A. EBSCO
   B. FirstSearch
   C. ProQuest
   D. Gale Group

23. What is the term for the blending of current and emerging technologies into a single multi-use device?

   A. Virtual reality
   B. Convergence
   C. Processing
   D. Artificial intelligence

24. Which of the following is an approach to interoperability that uses proxies as interfaces between existing systems?

   A. HotJava
   B. TeX
   C. InfoBus
   D. STARTS

25. The Metadata Object Description Schema, or MODS,   25.____
      I.   is an XML schema
     II.   was created by the Library of Congress for representing MARC-like semantics
    III.   can be used to carry selected data from MARC21 records
    IV.   cannot be used for the conversion of MARC to XML without loss of data

A.   I and II
B.   I, II and IV
C.   II and III
D.   I, II, III and IV

————

KEY (CORRECT ANSWERS)

1.	C		11.	B
2.	A		12.	C
3.	D		13.	B
4.	D		14.	C
5.	C		15.	A
6.	D		16.	B
7.	A		17.	D
8.	C		18.	B
9.	B		19.	B
10.	C		20.	A

21.	D
22.	B
23.	B
24.	C
25.	D

————

TEST 2

DIRECTIONS: Each question or incomplete statement is followed by several suggested answers or completions. Select the one that BEST answers the question or completes the statement. *PRINT THE LETTER OF THE CORRECT ANSWER IN THE SPACE AT THE RIGHT.*

1. The main advantage to using an intermediary service for access to electronic journals is that

    A. one search engine will search the contents of journals from several publishers and/ or disciplines
    B. the one-time start-up cost is predictable
    C. the databases will have citations and abstracts only for articles that are available in full-text
    D. the depth of backfiles is predictable

1._

2. A library automation system needs to be able to search compatible resources from a single interface, and to search text files based on keywords.
The standard query language that is used for this is

    A. WAIS
    B. Gopher
    C. ODBC
    D. Z39.50

2._

3. Under copyright law, the rights to publish a work in a form other than the original publication–for example, in installments in a periodical–are known as _____ rights.

    A. residual
    B. subsidiary
    C. site-specific
    D. residual

3._

4. _____ indexing is a method in which multiple concepts are combined by the indexer to form subject headings or descriptors assigned to documents dealing with complex subjects.

    A. Derivative
    B. Pre-coordinate
    C. String
    D. Post-coordinate

4._

5. Which of the following terms is associated with efforts to bridge the digital divide?

    A. E-rate
    B. Intellectual property
    C. Artificial intelligence
    D. Convergence

5._

6. After deciding to offer users online access to an electronic journals collection through the library's online catalog, a library must decide whether to use the "single-record" or "separate-record" approach to offering access to print and electronic versions. Advantages of the separate-record approach include the fact that it is

    I. better suited to handle linking relationships between formats
    II. it is prescribed by AACR2 (Anglo-American Cataloging Rules)
    III. used by the Government Printing Office (GPO)
    IV. preferred by the Cooperative Online Serials Program (CONSER)

    A. I only
    B. II and III
    C. I, II and IV
    D. I, II, III and IV

6._____

7. One of the key issues in remote access to library automated systems today is

    A. authentication
    B. free speech
    C. cost
    D. training

7._____

8. Which of the following is NOT a multiple-access database?

    A. A printed dictionary arranged alphabetically by headword
    B. A library catalog searchable by author, title, subject, and keywords
    C. A bibliographic database searchable by author, title, subject, or date
    D. A printed encyclopedia in alphabetical sections, with a subject or keyword index to the entire work at the end of the last volume.

8._____

9. Which of the following services is LEAST likely to be offered by a jobber?

    A. Approval plans
    B. Continuation orders
    C. Technical processing
    D. Online searchable bibliographies

9._____

10. Modern (5th generation) computers are most specifically characterized by the feature of

    A. transistors
    B. integrated chips
    C. multiprocessing
    D. data communications

10._____

11. In library acquisitions, a purchase order becomes a contract when

    A. the seller receives the invoice
    B. it is accepted by the purchaser
    C. the purchaser signs the invoice
    D. it is accepted by the seller

11._____

12. The primary metadata that describes a social science data set is a

    A. codebook   B. unicode
    C. chapbook   D. METS

12._____

13. The contents of a single CD-ROM are roughly equivalent to the contents of about _____ books.

    A. 15
    B. 120
    C. 300
    D. 250

14. Which of the following is NOT a link resolver?

    A. ICate
    B. PURL
    C. SFX
    D. Linkfinder Plus

15. Historical works are classified in the Library of Congress Classification System under the broad category designated

    A. L
    B. H
    C. D
    D. S

16. The most widely used medium for offline data storage is

    A. CD-ROM
    B. RAID
    C. DVD-ROM
    D. magnetic tape

17. In archives, the legal term for a record or document that is no longer in the possession of its original creator or legitimate custodian is

    A. dangler
    B. estray
    C. abductee
    D. orphan

18. The largest unit in a database is a

    A. file
    B. record
    C. subfield
    D. field

19. Which of the following is NOT typically part of an item record?

    A. Price
    B. Volume number
    C. Vendor
    D. Barcode

20. Which of the following is an advantage associated with the "scan-first" approach to pres-ervation-in which microfilm records are produced from digitized scans of original docu-ments? 20._____

    A. Wide range of equipment and service vendors
    B. Unsettled standards for preservation
    C. Adjustments can be made prior to conversion
    D. Higher image resolution than analog photography

21. Communications from an author to the editor of a journal typically do NOT include 21._____

    A. proof of permission
    B. referee comments
    C. article appropriate query
    D. copyright assignment

22. Which of the following is NOT a primary source? 22._____

    A. Memoir/autobiography
    B. Encyclopedia
    C. Minutes from an organization or agency
    D. Speech

23. A user initiates an online search by typing "author = Shakespeare." This is an example of a _____ search. 23._____

    A. fielded
    B. Boolean
    C. full-text
    D. stop-list

24. Asyndetic references or bibliographies 24._____

    A. lack descriptors
    B. include embedded hypertext
    C. focus on semantic relationships between topics
    D. lack cross-references

25. The most universally accepted criteria for weeding library items are based on 25._____

    A. subject area
    B. date of publication
    C. the condition or physical description of the item
    D. content

KEY (CORRECT ANSWERS)

1.	A	11.	D
2.	D	12.	A
3.	B	13.	C
4.	B	14.	B
5.	A	15.	C
6.	C	16.	D
7.	A	17.	B
8.	A	18.	A
9.	D	19.	C
10.	C	20.	C

21.	B
22.	B
23.	A
24.	D
25.	C

———

EXAMINATION SECTION
TEST 1

DIRECTIONS: Each question or incomplete statement is followed by several suggested answers or completions. Select the one that BEST answers the question or completes the statement. *PRINT THE LETTER OF THE CORRECT ANSWER IN THE SPACE AT THE RIGHT.*

1. What are the two major classification systems used in American libraries to organize library materials? 1._____

   A. Dewey Decimal and Library of Congress
   B. Dewey Decimal and OCLC
   C. Library of Congress and Universal Decimal
   D. Bliss Bibliographic and Cutter Expansive

2. The term _____ refers to creating a bibliographic record for an item using a record that has already been created by another library or organization. 2._____

   A. original cataloging
   B. archiving
   C. copy cataloging
   D. acquisitions

3. What is the primary purpose of a call number? 3._____

   A. Educate library patrons about library classification systems
   B. Prevent theft or misplacement of library materials
   C. Provide detailed subject and description information about an item
   D. Ensure items on the same subject are placed on the same shelf in the library

4. Which of the following would NOT be classified as a reference material? 4._____

   A. Atlas   B. Dictionary   C. Thesaurus   D. Fiction book

5. Which library department is responsible for ordering and receiving library materials? 5._____

   A. Acquisitions   B. Circulation   C. Reference   D. IT

6. Joni is assisting a patron who is a writer and is researching obscure information for a book. So far, Joni has been unable to find any materials at her library or other local libraries that meet the patron's needs.
Which of the following resources could Joni use to extend her search to libraries worldwide and increase her chances of locating materials for the patron? 6._____

   A. OCLC WorldCat
   B. AACR2
   C. EBSCOhost
   D. Millenium

7. Which of the following library materials would be classified as a serial?   7.____

    A. Compact disc
    B. DVD
    C. Magazine
    D. Non-fiction book

8. The Dewey Decimal system divides information into _____ main classes.   8.____

    A. 40   B. 20   C. 5   D. 10

9. Which of the following is NOT a function of OCLC?   9.____

    A. Enabling resource sharing
    B. Providing cataloging and metadata services
    C. Managing reader's advisory services
    D. Managing digital collection services

10. _____ is the principal cataloging code used to construct bibliographic descriptions for   10.____
library catalogs.

    A. OCLC
    B. AACR2
    C. MARC
    D. Gale

Questions 11-15.

DIRECTIONS: For questions 11 through 15, match the Dewey Decimal class in Column
                A to the corresponding class number in Column B.

Column A	Column B	
11. Language	A. 200	11.____
12. Social sciences	B. 300	12.____
13. Literature and rhetoric	C. 400	13.____
14. Religion	D. 800	14.____
15. History and geography	E. 900	15.____

16. Which of the following is NOT a task that is typically performed by the   16.____
reference department?

    A. administering fines
    B. reader's advisory
    C. assistance with online research
    D. preparation of research guides

17. What field is marked by the 020 tag in a MARC record?   17._____

   A. Library of Congress Control Number (LCCN)
   B. Personal name main entry
   C. International Standard Book Number (ISBN)
   D. Physical description

18. The purpose of a cutter number is to organize books by   18._____

   A. subject
   B. author's last name
   C. publisher
   D. genre

19. A(n) _____ search involves using the operators AND, OR, and NOT to link   19._____
   keywords and concepts.

   A. reader's advisory
   B. Boolean
   C. bibliographic
   D. index

20. Chelsea works at a public library and has the primary responsibility of   20._____
   suggesting fiction and non-fiction books to patrons based upon their interests
   and needs. In her position, Chelsea is providing _____ services.

   A. interlibrary loan
   B. acquisition
   C. reader's advisory
   D. collection management

21. Which of the following databases would be most useful for helping a patron find   21._____
   business and legal information?

   A. ERIC
   B. Medline
   C. NoveList
   D. LexisNexis

22. A(n) _____ record is a machine readable cataloging record, which means the   22._____
   information in the record can be interpreted by a computer.

   A. bibliographic control
   B. MARC
   C. ILL
   D. OCLC

23. A(n) _____ is a list of preferred terms used in an index or database.   23._____

    A. MARC record
    B. annotation
    C. abstract
    D. controlled vocabulary

24. What field is marked by the 100 tag in a MARC record?   24._____

    A. Title information
    B. Publication information
    C. Edition
    D. Personal name main entry

25. The first line in a Library of Congress call number is always a _____ line.   25._____

    A. whole number
    B. letter
    C. cutter
    D. date

_____

KEY (CORRECT ANSWERS)

1. A		11. C	
2. C		12. B	
3. D		13. D	
4. D		14. A	
5. A		15. E	
6. A		16. A	
7. C		17. C	
8. D		18. B	
9. C		19. B	
10. B		20. C	

21. D
22. B
23. D
24. D
25. B

_____

TEST 2

DIRECTIONS: Each question or incomplete statement is followed by several suggested answers or completions. Select the one that BEST answers the question or completes the statement. *PRINT THE LETTER OF THE CORRECT ANSWER IN THE SPACE AT THE RIGHT.*

1. The term _____ is used to refer to data about data.

   A. hypertext
   B. metadata
   C. subject heading
   D. serial

   1._____

2. Which of the following storage mediums typically has the longest archival lifespan?

   A. Books
   B. Flash drives
   C. CDs
   D. Microfilm

   2._____

3. In the Dewey Decimal System, what happens to class numbers as the subclass of the discipline becomes more specific?

   A. They begin to contain characters
   B. They begin to contain Roman numerals
   C. They become shorter
   D. They become longer

   3._____

4. The _____ classification system consists of 1 to 3 letters followed by 1 to 4 integers.

   A. Dewey Decimal
   B. Library of Congress
   C. Bliss Bibliographic
   D. Universal Decimal

   4._____

5. Which of the following is an example of a multi-subject database?

   A. LexisNexis
   B. ERIC
   C. Academic Search Premier
   D. AccessScience

   5._____

6. Which of the following is NOT an example of an access point?

   A. Author   B. Title   C. Subject heading   D. Due date

   6._____

7. Tamara works at a public library that uses the Dewey Decimal Classification system and she is cataloging a book about dog care. The author of the book is Karen Green. Which of the following call numbers should she assign to the book?

    A. 636.7 GRE
    B. SF 991. S6
    C. 391.5 GREEN
    D. BF 161. S4

7._____

8. _____ is a new cataloging standard based on the FRBR (functional requirements for bibliographic records) and FRAD (functional requirements for authority data) models.

    A. Resource Description and Access (RDA)
    B. OCLC Connexion
    C. Boolean logic
    D. Online Public Access Catalog (OPAC)

8._____

9. _____ maintains the largest database of bibliographic records in the world, as well as the information on which libraries own the items.

    A. Millennium   B. MARC   C. Sirius   D. OCLC

9._____

10. The term _____ refers to the items a library owns.

    A. depository   B. reserves   C. bindery   D. holdings

10._____

Questions 11-15

DIRECTIONS: In questions 11 through 15, match the Library of Congress class in Column A to the corresponding class letter in Column B.

Column A	Column B	
11. Fine Arts	A. J	11._____
12. Political Science	B. L	12._____
13. Agriculture	C. N	13._____
14. Military Science	D. S	14._____
15. Education	E. U	15._____

16. In a MARC record, each field is associated with a 3-digit number called a(n) _____.

16._____

    A. serial number
    B. tag
    C. indicator
    D. ISBN

17. Which of the following is NOT a guideline for performing a reference interview?   17._____

    A. Follow-up with the patron to make sure they have everything they need
    B. Keep the patron informed of your progress as you search
    C. Ask closed-ended questions
    D. Make eye contact

18. An International Standard Bibliographic Number (ISBN) has four parts.   18._____
    Which of the following is NOT one of these parts?

    A. Group identifier
    B. Page count
    C. Publisher identifier
    D. Check digit

19. In a MARC record, each indicator value is _____.   19._____

    A. a number from 0 to 9
    B. a number from 10 to 20
    C. a series of non-numerical characters
    D. one lowercase letter preceded by a delimiter

20. According to the American Library Association, the term _____ refers to the right of   20._____
    every individual to both seek and receive information from all points of view without
    restriction.

    A. censorship
    B. bibliographic control
    C. resource sharing
    D. intellectual freedom

Questions 21-25.

DIRECTIONS: In questions 21 through 25, match the MARC tag in Column A to the
             corresponding field in Column B.

Column A	Column B	
21. 245	A. topical subject heading	21._____
22. 250	B. title information	22._____
23. 260	C. physical description	23._____
24. 300	D. edition	24._____
25. 650	E. publication information	25._____

KEY (CORRECT ANSWERS)

1. B		11. C	
2. D		12. A	
3. D		13. D	
4. B		14. E	
5. C		15. B	
6. D		16. B	
7. A		17. C	
8. A		18. B	
9. D		19. A	
10. D		20. D	

21. B
22. D
23. E
24. C
25. A

_____

TEST 3

DIRECTIONS: Each question or incomplete statement is followed by several suggested answers or completions. Select the one that BEST answers the question or completes the statement. *PRINT THE LETTER OF THE CORRECT ANSWER IN THE SPACE AT THE RIGHT.*

1. Which of the following is a standard used for creating metadata?　　1._____

   A. Dublin Core
   B. OCLC
   C. ERIC
   D. Boolean logic

2. A brief summary of an article is known as a(n)　　2._____

   A. Database
   B. MARC record
   C. access point
   D. abstract

3. In a library, books that need repair are sent to the _____.　　3._____

   A. bindery
   B. labeler
   C. wholesaler
   D. accession supervisor

4. What is the primary purpose of interlibrary loan?　　4._____

   A. Increase communication between neighboring libraries
   B. Obtain materials for a patron which are not available at the patron's library
   C. Reduce the number of library materials which are damaged or missing
   D. Increase the uniformity of library cataloging records worldwide

5. Public records and historical documents would most likely be found in a library's　　5._____

   A. archives
   B. serials department
   C. AV department
   D. acquisitions department

6. Which of the following is NOT a type of subject heading list?　　6._____

   A. Library of Congress Subject Headings (LCSH)
   B. Sears List
   C. Cutter's Objects of the Catalog
   D. Faceted Application of Subject Terminology (FAST)

7. The term *OPAC* is often used to refer to a library's   7.____

   A. holdings
   B. classification system
   C. lending policy
   D. catalog

8. A(n) _____ is a subdivision of a more general subject heading.   8.____

   A. Index   B. abstract   C. subheading   D. holding

9. What does it mean when a library material is classified as non-circulating?   9.____

   A. The item is located in the library's archives
   B. The item can only be checked out for 24 hours
   C. The item cannot be checked out
   D. The item has not yet been cataloged

10. In a MARC record, subfield codes consist of _____.   10.____

   A. a number from 0 to 9
   B. a series of non-numerical characters
   C. a number from 10 to 20
   D. one lowercase letter, or sometimes a number, preceded by a delimiter

Questions 11-15.

DIRECTIONS: For questions 11 through 15, match the book topic in column A with the most appropriate Dewey Decimal call number in column B.

Column A	Column B	
11. Bipolar disorder	A. 746.46	11.____
12. Quilting	B. 512	12.____
13. Algebra	C. 940.54	13.____
14. Hinduism	D. 616.895	14.____
15. World War II	E. 294.5	15.____

16. Linus is a cataloger at a public library, and when he catalogs he chooses subject and name headings from the Library of Congress Subject Headings list. In this example, Linus is performing   16.____

   A. authority control
   B. indexing
   C. abstracting
   D. copy cataloging

17. The purpose of an abstract is to   17._____
   A. summarize content
   B. provide new information
   C. sort metadata
   D. offer in depth analysis of a subject

18. If a library removes a book from its shelves because one person or group disagrees   18._____
    with its content, this is an example of _____.

   A. intellectual freedom
   B. censorship
   C. reader's advisory
   D. plagiarism

19. Which of the following is NOT an example of a Boolean operator?   19._____

   A. and   B. or   C. but   D. not

20. Searching a database using "natural language" is referred to as   20._____
   A. Boolean logic
   B. indexing
   C. subject searching
   D. keyword searching

Questions 21-25.

DIRECTIONS: For questions 21 through 25, match the library-related term in column A
            with its correct meaning in column B.

Column A   Column B

21. overdue   A. setting an item aside for a patron   21._____
22. renewal   B. an item that has not been returned by the due date   22._____
23. hold   C. a publication issued on a regular basis   23._____
24. periodical   D. section of the library containing the circulating book collection   24._____
25. stacks   E. extending the loan period of an item   25._____

_____

KEY (CORRECT ANSWERS)

1.	A	11.	D
2.	D	12.	A
3.	A	13.	B
4.	B	14.	E
5.	A	15.	C
6.	C	16.	A
7.	D	17.	A
8.	C	18.	B
9.	C	19.	C
10.	D	20.	D

21.	B
22.	E
23.	A
24.	C
25.	D

_____

TEST 4

DIRECTIONS: Each question or incomplete statement is followed by several suggested answers or completions. Select the one that BEST answers the question or completes the statement. *PRINT THE LETTER OF THE CORRECT ANSWER IN THE SPACE AT THE RIGHT.*

1. When a library book has a size designation of quarto this indicates that its height   1._____

   A. exceeds 42 cm or its length exceeds 35 cm
   B. and length are proportionate
   C. is less than 20 cm and its length is more than 20 cm
   D. is between 29 and 42 cm, or its length is between 25 and 35 cm

2. Leah has requested a book for a patron from an out-of-state library using OCLC. The   2._____
   next day, while looking at the request in OCLC Request Manager, she notices that
   status of her request has been changed from "pending" to "conditional."
   What does this new status indicate about Leah's request?

   A. The lender is unwilling to send the item
   B. The lender has stated conditions for lending in the lending notes
   C. The lender has not yet viewed the request
   D. The lender has sent the item

3. When creating a call number, the cutter number is usually based on the _____, while   3._____
   the work mark is usually based on the _____.

   A. title; main entry
   B. publication date; main entry
   C. main entry; title
   D. title; publication date

4. Which of the following is NOT a guideline for shelving books by call number?   4._____

   A. File one decimal place at a time
   B. Ordering is based on the guideline "nothing before something"
   C. File one numerical place at a time after each capital letter
   D. File groups of letters together when they follow numbers

5. _____, which is being utilized by many libraries, refers to technologies that use radio   5._____
   waves to automatically identify different items.

   A. RDA   B. OCLC   C. RFID   D. WorldCat

6. Which of the following has no significance other than being a distinctive and definite identifier?

   6._____

   A. ISBN
   B. Call number
   C. Subfield code in a MARC record
   D. ISSN

7. According to the Child Internet Protection Act (CIPA), public libraries that receive federal assistance are required to

   7._____

   A. install filters on all computers
   B. visually monitor the internet use of all patrons
   C. provide separate computer stations for children
   D. deny internet access to minors

8. A(n) _____ includes its author's name, title, publisher and place of publication, and date of publication.

   8._____

   A. ISSN
   B. citation to a book
   C. call number
   D. index entry

9. In which of the following scenarios would a library be infringing on copyright law?

   9._____

   A. It charges a nominal fee for the use of videos
   B. It knowingly lends videos to a patron using them for a public performance
   C. It does not label videos with a copyright warning statement
   D. It sells its used videos in its annual book sale

10. An electronic version of a book that can be read on a computer or mobile device is known as a(n)

   10._____

   A. e-reserve
   B. flash drive
   C. ILL
   D. e-book

11. Carol is a reference librarian and often provides reference services to patrons remotely via chat, email, instant-messaging and video conferencing.
This type of reference service is known as

   11._____

   A. reader's advisory
   B. proctoring
   C. virtual reference
   D. the open web

12. Thomas is a reference librarian and is trying to help a patron find a primary source   12._____
about the Holocaust. Which of the following sources would be sufficient?

    A. *The Diary of Anne Frank*
    B. A biography of Adolf Hitler
    C. The film *Schindler's List*
    D. A Wikipedia entry on the Holocaust

13. When library patrons have the ability to log onto library resources like databases   13._____
from an off-site location, it is known as

    A. authentication
    B. remote access
    C. virtual reference
    D. telecommuting

14. Which of the following is NOT a type of AV material?   14._____

    A. Films
    B. Slides
    C. Records
    D. Magazines

15. How do the physical descriptions of audiovisual items in MARC records differ from   15._____
that of books?

    A. They are much longer
    B. They only contain alphanumeric codes
    C. They are much shorter
    D. They must be composed in complete sentences

Questions 16-20.

DIRECTIONS: For questions 16 through 20, match the OCLC interlibrary loan request
status in column A with its correct meaning in column B.

Column A   Column B

16. Received   A. the lender wants you to return the item immediately   16._____
17. In Process   B. no lender could supply the item prior to the Need Before date   17._____
18. Unfilled   C. you have already reviewed these requests   18._____
19. Expired   D. the borrower received the item from the lender   19._____
20. Recalled   E. no lender could supply the item   20._____

21. Which of the following is NOT one of the advantages of using MARC records?   21._____

   A. They allow libraries to better share bibliographic resources
   B. They prevent duplication of work
   C. They provide cataloging data that is unique and interesting
   D. They foster communication of information

22. In a MARC record, a blank, or undefined, indicator position is represented by which   22._____
   of the following characters?

   A. #   B. &   C. @   D. %

23. Which of the following is NOT considered a content designator in a MARC record?   23._____

   A. Tags   B. Indicators   C. Cutter numbers   D. Subfield codes

24. In a MARC record, which fields have no subfields?   24._____

   A. Only fields 001 and 002
   B. Only fields 003 and 004
   C. Fields 100 through 600
   D. Fields 001 through 009

25. A(n) _____ is a list of names, places and subjects that tells you where those names,   25._____
   places or subjects are discussed within a publication.

   A. biography   B. periodical   C. index   D. catalog

_____

KEY (CORRECT ANSWERS)

1. D	11. C	21. C
2. B	12. A	22. A
3. C	13. B	23. C
4. D	14. D	24. D
5. C	15. A	25. C
6. D	16. D	
7. A	17. C	
8. B	18. E	
9. B	19. B	
10. D	20. A	

_____

EXAMINATION SECTION
TEST 1

DIRECTIONS: Each question or incomplete statement is followed by several suggested answers or completions. Select the one that BEST answers the question or completes the statement. *PRINT THE LETTER OF THE CORRECT ANSWER IN THE SPACE AT THE RIGHT.*

1. An employee requests a book which is not in the department library.
   Of the following, the MOST advisable course of action for you to take is to

   A. attempt to get the book for him by means of the department's affiliation with the public library
   B. explain that the book is not available from the department's library
   C. suggest that he try his local public library and give him a list of local libraries
   D. tell him where he may purchase the book and offer to make the purchase for him

   1.____

2. The catalog for the use of department employees has just been thoroughly checked and revised by a professional librarian. After trying to find the name of a book in the catalog, an employee tells you that he cannot find it.
   Of the following, the MOST advisable action for you to take FIRST is to

   A. call the public library for the exact title
   B. look it up in the catalog yourself
   C. look through the stacks for the book
   D. tell him you are sorry but the book is not in the department library

   2.____

3. You find that three pages are missing from one of the copies of a very popular book in the department library.
   Of the following, the MOST advisable action for you to take is to

   A. discard the book since its usefulness is now sharply curtailed
   B. order another copy of the book but keep the old copy until the new one is received
   C. report the fact to the head of the department and request further instructions
   D. type copies of the pages from another volume of the book and tape them in the appropriate place

   3.____

4. The department library is scheduled to close at 5 P.M. It is now 4:55, and an employee reading a book shows no signs of leaving.
   Of the following, the MOST advisable action for you to take is to

   A. tell him it is time to leave
   B. tell him the time and ask him if he wishes to borrow the book
   C. turn the lights off and on, indirectly suggesting that he leave
   D. wait until he decides to leave

   4.____

5. The dealer from whom you have been buying books for the department library has informed you that henceforth he can give you only a fifteen percent instead of a twenty percent discount.
   Of the following, the MOST advisable course of action for you to take FIRST is to

   5.____

A. accept the fifteen percent discount
B. inform the head of your department
C. investigate the discount given by other book dealers
D. order directly from the publishers

6. Your supervisor is a professional librarian and is responsible for the selection of material to be added to the department library in which you are an employee. Shortly after you start on the job, an employee of the department brings you a written request to have several books of his choice added to the library.
Of the following, the MOST advisable course of action for you to take is to

A. order the books immediately
B. pass the suggestion along to your supervisor
C. refuse to accept his suggestion
D. tell him that he will have to buy the books

7. You object to your supervisor's plan to change the system in the department library from closed to open stacks.
Of the following, the MOST advisable course of action for you to take is to

A. ask other members of the staff to support your objections
B. await further instructions and then do as you are told
C. discuss your objections with your supervisor
D. send a brief report of your objections to the department head

8. Two weeks after you begin working in the department library, you learn that books in library bindings last twice as long as those with the publishers' bindings.
Of the following, the MOST advisable course of action for you to follow is to

A. buy only paperbound books
B. have all new books put in library bindings
C. put in library bindings only rare editions
D. put in library bindings only those books likely to get hard use

9. Your superior is away on an official trip. You have been asked to type and e-mail several hundred letters before he returns. Just as you begin the job, the computer breaks down.
Of the following, the MOST advisable course of action for you to take is to

A. arrange to have the computer serviced as soon as possible
B. write the letters by hand
C. postpone the job until after your supervisor returns
D. write to your supervisor for advice

10. Your supervisor in the department library is out for the day. You receive a telephone call from another city department asking if they may borrow one of the books in your library.
Of the following, the MOST advisable action for you to take FIRST is to tell the department

A. that books are not permitted out of the department
B. that you will check and call back the next day
C. to send a representative to inquire the next day
D. to write a letter to the department head

11. Two months have passed since the head of the department has borrowed one of the books in the department library. Of the following, the MOST advisable action for you to take is to

   A. ask the department head if he wishes to keep the book out longer
   B. leave a note for the department head telling him that the book should be returned immediately
   C. wait another month and then write the book off as lost
   D. wait until you receive another request for the book

11.____

12. Your supervisor tells you that he would like to have all old book cards replaced, all torn pages mended, and the books put in good condition in all other respects by the following day. You know that this is an impossible task.
   Of the following, the MOST advisable course of action for you to take is to

   A. attempt to finish as much of the job as possible
   B. explain the difficulties involved to the supervisor and await further instruction
   C. ignore the request since it is completely unreasonable
   D. make a complaint to the head of the department

12.____

13. The library in which you work has received about fifty new books. These books must be cataloged, but you have had no experience in this type of work. However, you have been told that a professional librarian will join the staff in about six weeks.
   Of the following, the MOST advisable course of action for you to take in the meantime is to

   A. close the library for a week and try to do the cataloging yourself
   B. lend the books only to those who can get special permission
   C. let the users take the books even though they are not cataloged
   D. put all the books in storage until they can be cataloged

13.____

14. The hospital library in which you work has a large back-log of books that need to be mended. You are unable to do more than a small part of the job by yourself. One of the patients in the hospital has done book binding and mending. He offers to help you because he sees the need for doing the job and because he wants something to do with his hands.
   Of the following, the MOST advisable course of action for you to take is to

   A. accept his offer on condition that the doctor approves
   B. ask him to push the book cart around the wards so you will be free to do the mending
   C. refuse his offer
   D. write a letter to his former employer to find out whether he is a good bookbinder

14.____

15. You accidentally spill a glass of water over an open book.
   Of the following, the MOST advisable action for you to take FIRST in most cases is to

   A. discard the book to prevent the water from spoiling other material
   B. hang the book up by its binding
   C. press the covers together to squeeze out the water
   D. separate the wet pages with blotters

15.____

16. In mending a book, you overturn a jar of glue on a new book.   16.
    Of the following, the MOST advisable action for you to take FIRST is to

    A. allow the glue to harden so that it may be peeled off
    B. attempt to wipe off the glue with any clean scrap paper
    C. discard the book to prevent other materials from being spoiled
    D. report the incident immediately to your supervisor

17. Of the following, the situation LEAST likely to result in injury to books is one in which   17.

    A. all books support each other standing upright
    B. short books are placed between tall ones
    C. the books are as close together as possible
    D. the books lean against the sides of the shelves

18. Of the following, a damp cloth may BEST be used to clean a cloth book cover that has   18.
    been coated with

    A. benzene   B. gold leaf
    C. turpentine   D. varnish

19. Decay of leather bindings may be MOST effectively delayed by   19.

    A. a short tanning period
    B. air conditioning
    C. rubbing periodically with a damp cloth
    D. treatment with heat

20. When paste is used to mend a page, it is MOST desirable that the page should then be   20.

    A. aired   B. heated   C. pressed   D. sprayed

21. A book that is perfectly clean but has been used by someone with chicken pox can prob-   21.
    ably BEST be handled by

    A. burning, followed by proper disposal of the ashes
    B. forty-eight hour exposure to ultraviolet light
    C. keeping it out of circulation for six months
    D. treating it the same as any other book

22. The BEST combination of temperature and humidity for books is temperature _____   22.
    degrees, humidity _____.

    A. 50-60; 20-30%   B. 60-70; 10-20%
    C. 60-70; 50-60%   D. 70-80; 70-80%

23. When a new book is received, it is LEAST important to keep a record of the   23.

    A. author's name
    B. cost of the book
    C. number of pages
    D. source from which it was obtained

24.	You have just received from the publisher a new book for the department library, but you find that the binding is torn.
Of the following, the MOST advisable action for you to take is to   24._____

	A.	mend the binding and take no further action
	B.	mend the binding but claim a price discount
	C.	report the damage to the department head
	D.	send the book back to the publisher

25.	Of the following, a characteristic of MOST photographic charging systems is that 25._____

	A.	book cards are not used
	B.	charging is done by one person
	C.	date due is stamped on borrower's card
	D.	transaction cards are not used

———

KEY (CORRECT ANSWERS)

1.	A	11.	A
2.	B	12.	B
3.	D	13.	C
4.	B	14.	A
5.	C	15.	D
6.	B	16.	B
7.	C	17.	A
8.	D	18.	D
9.	A	19.	B
10.	B	20.	C

21.	D
22.	C
23.	C
24.	D
25.	B

TEST 2

DIRECTIONS: Each question or incomplete statement is followed by several suggested answers or completions. Select the one that BEST answers the question or completes the statement. *PRINT THE LETTER OF THE CORRECT ANSWER IN THE SPACE AT THE RIGHT.*

1. In a card catalog, a reference from one subject heading to another is MOST commonly called a(n) _____ reference.

    A. cross   B. direct   C. primary   D. indirect

1.__

2. A book which is shortened by omission of detail but which retains the general sense of the original is called a(n)

    A. compendium   B. manuscript
    C. miniature   D. abridgment

2.__

3. An anonymous book is a

    A. book published before 1500
    B. book whose author is unknown
    C. copy which is defective
    D. work that is out of print

3.__

4. All the letters, figures, and symbols assigned to a book to indicate its location on library shelves comprise the _____ number.

    A. call   B. Cutter   C. index   D. inventory

4.__

5. The term *format* does NOT refer to a book's

    A. binding   B. size
    C. theme   D. typography

5.__

6. The term *card catalog* USUALLY refers to a

    A. catalog consisting of loose-leaf pages upon which the cards are pasted
    B. catalog in which entries are on separate cards arranged in a definite order
    C. catalog of the cards available from the Library of Congress
    D. record on cards of the works which have been weeded out of the library collection

6.__

7. The term *circulation record* USUALLY refers to a record of

    A. daily attendance
    B. the books borrowed
    C. the most popular books
    D. the books out on interlibrary loan

7.__

8. Reading shelves USUALLY involves checking the shelves to see that all the books

    A. are in the correct order
    B. are suitable for the library's patrons
    C. are there
    D. have been cataloged correctly

8.__

9. In an alphabetical catalog of book titles and authors' names, the name *de Santis* would be filed

    A. after *DeWitt*
    B. after *Sanders*
    C. before AND THEN THERE WERE NONE
    D. before *Deutsch*

9.____

10. In typing, the Shift key on the computer keyboard is used to

    A. change the font size
    B. indent a line of text
    C. type numbers
    D. type capitals

10.____

11. The abbreviation e.g. means *most nearly*

    A. as follows   B. for example
    C. refer to   D. that is

11.____

12. The abbreviation ff. means *most nearly*

    A. and following pages   B. formerly
    C. frontispiece   D. the end

12.____

13. The abbreviation ibid, means *most nearly*

    A. consult the index   B. in the same place
    C. see below   D. turn the page

13.____

14. *Ex libris* is a Latin phrase meaning

    A. former librarian   B. from the books
    C. without charge   D. without liberty

14.____

15. An expurgated edition of a book is one which

    A. contains many printing errors
    B. includes undesirable passages
    C. is not permitted in public libraries
    D. omits objectionable material

15.____

16. The re-charging of a book to a borrower is USUALLY called

    A. fining   B. processing
    C. reissue   D. renewal

16.____

17. A sheet of paper that is pierced with holes is

    A. borated   B. collated
    C. perforated   D. serrated

17.____

18. *Glossary* means *most nearly* a(n)

    A. dictionary of selected terms in a particular book or field
    B. list of chapter headings in the order in which they appear in a book
    C. section of the repairing division which coats books with a protective lacquer
    D. alphabetical table of the contents of a book

18.____

19. *Accessioning* means *most nearly*

    A. acquiring books
    B. arranging books for easy access
    C. donating books as gifts
    D. listing books in the order of purchase

20. *Bookplate* means *most nearly*

    A. a label in a book showing who owns it
    B. a metal device for holding books upright
    C. a rounded zinc surface upon which a page is printed
    D. the flat part of the binding of a book

21. *Thesaurus* means *most nearly* a book which

    A. contains instructions on how to prepare a thesis
    B. contains words grouped according to similarity of meaning
    C. describes the techniques of dramatic acting
    D. gives quotations from well-known works of literature

22. *Salacious* means *most nearly*

    A. careful   B. delicious   C. lewd   D. salty

23. *Pseudonym* means *most nearly*

    A. false report   B. fictitious name
    C. libelous statement   D. psychic phenomenon

24. *Gamut* means *most nearly* a(n)

    A. bookworm   B. simpleton
    C. vagrant   D. entire range

25. *Monograph* means *most nearly* a

    A. machine for duplicating typewritten material by means of a stencil
    B. picture reproduced on an entire page of a manuscript
    C. single chart used to represent statistical data
    D. systematic treatise on a particular subject

19.__
20.__
21.__
22.__
23.__
24.__
25.__

KEY (CORRECT ANSWERS)

1.	A		11.	B
2.	D		12.	A
3.	B		13.	B
4.	A		14.	B
5.	C		15.	D
6.	B		16.	D
7.	B		17.	C
8.	A		18.	A
9.	D		19.	D
10.	D		20.	A

21.	B
22.	C
23.	B
24.	D
25.	D

———

TEST 3

DIRECTIONS: Each question or incomplete statement is followed by several suggested answers or completions. Select the one that BEST answers the question or completes the statement. *PRINT THE LETTER OF THE CORRECT ANSWER IN THE SPACE AT THE RIGHT.*

Questions 1-15.

DIRECTIONS: Questions 1 through 15 are to be answered SOLELY on the basis of the information contained in the following passage.

Machines may be useful for bibliographic purposes, but they will be useful only if we study the bibliographic requirements to be met and the machines available, in terms of each Job which needs to be done. Many standard tools now available are more efficient than high-speed machines if the machines are used as gadgets rather than as the mechanical elements of well-considered systems.

It does not appear impossible for us to learn to think in terms of scientific management to such an extent that we may eventually be able to do much of the routine part of bibliographic work mechanically with greater efficiency, both in terms of cost per unit of service and in terms of management of the intellectual content of literature. There are many bibliographic tasks which will probably not be done mechanically in the near future because the present tools appear to present great advantages over any machine in sight; for example, author bibliography done on the electronic machines would appear to require almost as much work in instructing the machine as is required to look in an author catalog. The major field of usefulness of the machines would appear to be that of subject bibliography, and particularly in research rather than quick reference jobs.

Machines now available or in sight cannot answer a quick reference question either as fast or as economically as will consultation of standard reference works such as dictionaries, encyclopedias, or almanacs, nor would it appear worthwhile to instruct a machine and run the machine to pick out one recent book or "any recent book" in a broad subject field. It would appear, therefore, that high-speed electronic or electrical machinery may be used for bibliographic purposes only in research institutions, at least for the next five or ten years, and their use will probably be limited to research problems in those institutions. It seems quite probable that during the next decade electronic machines, including the Rapid Selector, which was designed with bibliographic purposes in mind, will find application in administrative, office, and business uses to a much greater extent than they will in bibliographic operations.

The shortcomings of machines used as gadgets have been stressed in this paper. Nevertheless, the use of machines for bibliographic purposes is developing, and it is developing rapidly. It appears quite certain that several of the machines and mechanical devices can now perform certain of the routine operations involved in bibliographic work more accurately and more efficiently than these operations can be performed without them.

At least one machine, the Rapid Selector, appears potentially capable of performing higher orders of bibliographic work than we have been able to perform in the past, if and when we learn: (a) what is really needed for the advancement of learning in the way of bibliographic services; and (b) how to utilize the machine efficiently.

There is no magic in machines as such. There will be time-lag in their application, just as there was with the typewriter. The speed and efficiency in handling the mechanical part of bibliographic work, which will determine the point of diminishing returns, depend in large measure on how long it will be before we approach these problems from the point of view of scientific management.

This report cannot solve the problem of bibliographic organization. Machines alone cannot solve the problem. We need to develop systems of handling the mass of bibliographic material, but such systems cannot be developed until we discover and establish our objectives, our plans, our standards, our methods and controls, within the framework of each situation. This may take twenty years or it may take one hundred, but it will come. The termination of how long the time-lag will be rests upon our time-lag in gathering objective information upon which scientific management of literature can be based.

1. On the basis of the above passage, machines will *probably* be MOST useful in   1._____

    A. determining the cost per unit of service
    B. quick reference jobs
    C. subject bibliography
    D. title cataloging

2. On the basis of the above passage, the Rapid Selector will *probably* be LEAST used during the next ten years in   2._____

    A. administration   B. bibliographic work
    C. business   D. office work

3. It may be inferred from the above passage that is is NOT practical to use machines to do author bibliography because   3._____

    A. experienced machine operators are not available
    B. more than one machine is needed for such a task
    C. the results obtained from a machine are unreliable
    D. too much work is involved in instructing the machine

4. On the basis of the above passage, one of the criteria of efficiency is the   4._____

    A. amount of work required   B. cost per unit of service
    C. net cost of service   D. number of machines available

5. On the basis of the above passage, the LEAST efficient of the following for quick reference jobs are   5._____

    A. bibliographies   B. dictionaries
    C. encyclopedias   D. machines

6. On the basis of the above passage, in the next few years, high-speed electronic machinery will probably be used for bibliographic purposes only by   6._____

    A. civil engineers
    B. institutions of higher education
    C. publishers
    D. research institutions

7. On the basis of the above passage, the Rapid Selector was designed for use in handling   7.__

     A. bibliographic operations
     B. computing problems
     C. photographic reproduction
     D. standard reference works

8. On the basis of the above passage, progress on the development of machines to do bib-   8.__
liographic tasks has reached the point at which

     A. all present tools have become obsolete
     B. certain jobs are better performed with machines than without them
     C. machines are as efficient in doing quick reference jobs as in doing special research
        jobs
     D. machines are no longer regarded as being too expensive

9. The one of the following which is NOT stated by the above passage to be essential in   9.__
developing ways of handling bibliographic material is

     A. discovering methods and controls
     B. establishing objectives
     C. establishing standards
     D. obtaining historical data

10. The above passage indicates that machines alone will NOT be able to solve the problem   10.__
of

     A. bibliographic organization
     B. reference work
     C. scientific management
     D. system analysis

11. On the basis of the above passage, the viewpoint of scientific management is essential in   11.__

     A. developing the mechanical handling of bibliographic work
     B. operating the Rapid Selector
     C. repairing electronic machines
     D. showing that people are always superior to machines in bibliographic work

12. On the basis of the above passage, there are machines in existence which   12.__

     A. are particularly useful for statistical analysis in library work
     B. are the result of scientific management of bibliographic work
     C. have not been efficiently utilized for bibliographic work
     D. may be installed in a medium-sized library

13. On the basis of the above passage, the scientific management of literature awaits the   13.__

     A. assembling of objective information
     B. compilation of new reference books
     C. development of more complex machines
     D. development of simplified machinery

14. Based on the above passage, it may be INFERRED that the author's attitude toward the   14._____
    use of machines in bibliographic work is that they

    A. have limited usefulness at the present time
    B. will become useful only if scientific management is applied
    C. will probably always be restricted to routine operations
    D. will probably never be useful

15. The author of the above passage believes that high-speed machines are BEST adapted   15._____
    to bibliographic work when they are used

    A. as gadgets
    B. in place of standard reference works
    C. to perform complex operations
    D. to perform routine operations

Questions 16-25.

DIRECTIONS: Questions 16 through 25 deal with the classification of non-fiction books
             according to the Dewey Classification as outlined below. For each book listed,
             print in the space on the right the letter in front of the class to which it belongs.

<u>Classification</u>

16.	Ernst. WORDS: ENGLISH ROOTS AND HOW THEY GROW	A.	000 General Works	16._____	
17.	Faulkner. FROM VERSAILLES TO THE NEW DEAL	B.	100 Philosophy	17._____	
18.	Fry. CHINESE ART	C.	200 Religion	18._____	
19.	Kant. CRITIQUE OF PURE REASON	D.	300 Social Science	19._____	
20.	Millikan. THE ELECTRON	E.	400 Philology	20._____	
21.	Morgan. THEORY OF THE GENE	F.	500 Pure Science	21._____	
22.	Raine. THE YEAR ONE; POEMS	G.	600 Applied Science, Useful Arts	22._____	
23.	Richards. PRINCIPLES OF LITERARY CRITICISM	H.	700 Fine Arts	23._____	
24.	Steinberg. BASIC JUDAISM	I.	800 Literature, Belleslettres	24._____	
25.	Strachey. QUEEN VICTORIA	J.	900 History, Biography	25._____	

KEY (CORRECT ANSWERS)

1.	C		11.	A
2.	B		12.	C
3.	D		13.	A
4.	B		14.	A
5.	D		15.	D
6.	D		16.	E
7.	A		17.	J
8.	B		18.	H
9.	D		19.	B
10.	A		20.	F

21.	F
22.	I
23.	I
24.	C
25.	J

———

EXAMINATION SECTION
TEST 1

DIRECTIONS: Each question or incomplete statement is followed by several suggested answers or completions. Select the one that BEST answers the question or completes the statement. *PRINT THE LETTER OF THE CORRECT ANSWER IN THE SPACE AT THE RIGHT.*

1. The MOST popular format for a library catalog in the United States is the   1.____

    A. Union list   B. Card catalog   C. C.B.I.
    D. MARC catalog   E. Sears catalog

2. The *two most usual* arrangements for library catalogs are _____ catalogs.   2.____

    A. dictionary and accessioned   B. classified and divided
    C. dictionary and divided   D. numerical and divided
    E. dictionary and classified

3. An example of a book catalog is   3.____

    A. C.B.I.   B. the Dewey Decimal System
    C. the National Union Catalog   D. Reader's Guide
    E. P.A.I.S.

4. *Most* library materials are shelved by   4.____

    A. classification number order   B. numerical order
    C. accession number   D. shelf list number
    E. size of particular format

5. To maintain the library collection in good order, it is necessary to check the arrangement of materials on the shelf regularly.
This is called   5.____

    A. shelf listing   B. classifying
    C. shelf checking   D. shelf reading
    E. shelf revision

6. A bibliography is a   6.____

    A. catalog   B. union list
    C. list of materials   D. accession list
    E. series of footnotes

7. A reference from one subject heading to another is usually referred to as a   7.____

    A. citation   B. referral   C. cross reference
    D. primary reference   E. secondary reference

8. The circulation record in a library usually refers to the   8.____

    A. number of patrons per day
    B. circulation of materials within the library
    C. number of materials borrowed
    D. number of materials purchased
    E. number of staff at circulation desk

9.   A microfirm is a reproduction, greatly reduced in size, of   9.___

    A.   alphanumeric matter
    B.   graphic matter
    C.   nonprint beta forms
    D.   realia or alphanumeric matter
    E.   alphanumeric or graphic matter

10.   A fiche is a sheet of film *usually* _____ inches.   10.___

    A. 3 x 5   B. 5 x 7   C. 4 x 6   D. 8 x 10   E. 2 x 3

11.   Microcard can reproduce up to _____ pages.   11.___

    A. 28   B. 48   C. 94   D. 106   E. 120

12.   Microprint can reproduce up to _____ pages.   12.___

    A. 28   B. 48   C. 94   D. 106   E. 120

13.   When a work is revised in the same format, the revised work is usually referred to as a   13.___

    A. new publication   B. new issuance
    C. new edition   D. revised version
    E. latest imprint

14.   Imprint consists of   14.___

    A. place of publisher, edition
    B. place of publisher, name of publisher, distributor, date of copyright
    C. place of publisher, date of copyright, credentials of author
    D. date of copyright, edition
    E. place of publisher, name of publisher, distributor, date of copyright edition

15.   Copyright date indicates the year in which   15.___

    A. a work is initiated
    B. a work is terminated
    C. authorized copies of a work are first made available to the public
    D. authorized copies of a work are sent to the printer
    E. the work was approved by the publisher

16.   Color coding of catalog cards usually indicates that material is   16.___

    A. on reserve
    B. available for inter-library loan
    C. in an audio-visual format
    D. geared to young adults
    E. in reference section

17.   A transparency is an image or transparent material designed to be used with a(n)   17.___

    A. opaque projector   B. diazo projector
    C. overhead projector   D. ektagraphic visual maker
    E. movie projector

18. Realia refers to   18.____

    A. multi-media kits   B. C.A.I.   C. intergrams
    D. maps   E. real things

19. Accession number refers to   19.____

    A. copyright date   B. edition
    C. order of acquisition   D. order on shelf
    E. order of cataloging

20. The combination of numbers and letters which indicates the classification of a work and   20.____
its location on the shelf is the _____ number.

    A. letter   B. accession   C. shelf-list
    D. call   E. Dewey

21. An extremely brief summary of the content of a work is usually referred to as a(n)   21.____

    A. evaluation   B. review   C. blurb
    D. annotation   E. precis

22. OCLC provides   22.____

    A. national film rental service
    B. cataloging in publication
    C. local film rental services
    D. C.A.I.
    E. centralized bibliographic and reference services

23. To obtain reviews of a popular work of fiction, the MOST appropriate source would be   23.____

    A. P.A.I.S.
    B. Book Review Digest
    C. Reader's Guide
    D. a comprehensive book review source
    E. Booklist

24. The two common forms of videotape used in today's libraries are: 24.____

    A. ASA and TWK   B. VHS and ASA   C. BETA and ASA
    D. VHS and BETA   E. TWK and PHILIPS

25. The physical description of a work which guides the user in the selection of any equip-   25.____
ment which may be necessary to utilize the material is the

    A. creator main entry   B. collation
    C. imprint   D. description
    E. continuation card

26. A permanently encased film or tape is also referred to as a   26.____

    A. realia   B. cassette   C. super-8
    D. diorama   E. filmstrip

27. Incunabula refer to

    A. books printed before 1600
    B. books printed after 1600
    C. musical compositions of the 14th century
    D. books printed before 1500
    E. books printed after 1500

27._

28. Original manuscripts, contemporary records, or documents which are ready by an author in writing a book, are MOST commonly referred to as

    A. reference materials
    B. classified sources
    C. secondary sources
    D. bibliography
    E. primary sources

28._

29. A printed blank on which one enters the author, title, and call number for a book is *usually* referred to as a _____ slip.

    A. patron's
    B. user's
    C. call
    D. request
    E. borrower's

29._

30. The use of selected readings and related materials for therapeutic purposes in physical medicine and in mental health is referred to as

    A. bibliothetic
    B. bibliothecary
    C. bibliotherapy
    D. medical librarianship
    E. medical therapy

30._

31. An index in periodical form which combines successively the entries of earlier issues or volumes into a single index is *usually* referred to as a(n) _____ index.

    A. progressive
    B. ongoing
    C. sequential
    D. cumulative
    E. reviewing

31._

32. Books intended for the general public and marketed to librarians are *usually* referred to as _____ editions.

    A. general
    B. commercial
    C. trade
    D. special
    E. first

32._

33. Information on a main entry catalog card giving the other headings under which the work is listed is referred to as the

    A. imprint
    B. tracing
    C. collation
    D. listing
    E. indention

33._

34. A computer designed to accomplish one specific task or set of tasks is referred to as a(n) _____ computer.

    A. special-purpose
    B. soft-wired
    C. IBM special
    D. task-oriented
    E. Selectric

34._

35. A storage technique which releases data stored at any location in the memory of a computer almost as quickly as data stored at any other location is referred to as _____ storage.

    A. specific-access
    B. remote-access
    C. tandom-access
    D. varied-access
    E. multi-access

35._

36. The journal of the American book industry founded in 1872 which provides current news and reports on trends, companies, persons, and business activities related to the profession of books is

    A. Wilson Library Bulletin   B. Booklist
    C. American Libraries   D. Library Journal
    E. Publishers Weekly

36.____

37. An assumed name or nom de plume is a(n)

    A. proofreader   B. editor   C. pseudonym
    D. given name   E. author

37.____

38. A treatise on *one* particular subject is *usually* referred to as a(n)

    A. article   B. paper   C. book
    D. monograph   E. festschrift

38.____

39. An edition of a volume or a set of volumes of which a stated number of copies is printed is *usually* referred to as a

    A. limited edition   B. festschrift
    C. monograph   D. special publication
    E. library edition

39.____

40. Publishers' overstocks of titles offered at reduced prices through jobbers and booksellers are *usually* referred to as

    A. special editions   B. overstocks
    C. reissues   D. reprints
    E. remainders

40.____

41. ALA's monthly news magazine is entitled

    A. Library Journal
    B. American Libraries
    C. American Library Association Journal
    D. Library Bulletin
    E. Library Association News

41.____

42. AECT's monthly news magazine is entitled

    A. Journal of Instructional Development
    B. Audiovisual Instruction
    C. Instructional Innovator
    D. AV news
    E. Instructional Technology

42.____

43. Discarding books from a library's collection is *usually* referred to as

    A. revising   B. thinning   C. updating
    D. weeding   E. eliminating

43.____

44. Britannica and Collier's are

    A. dictionaries   B. encyclopedias   C. handbooks
    D. almanacs   E. atlases

44.____

45. INFORMATION PLEASE and WHITAKER'S are   45.___

    A. directories   B. encyclopedias   C. handbooks
    D. almanacs   E. atlases

46. Funk and Wagnalls and Webster's are BEST known for   46.___

    A. dictionaries   B. almanacs   C. directories
    D. atlases   E. encyclopedias

47. C.B.I. *most commonly* refers to   47.___

    A. Current Book Information
    B. Cumulative Book Index
    C. Complete Book Indices
    D. Cumulative Book Information
    E. Complete Book Index

48. When one library lends its materials to another, the procedure is *usually* referred to as   48.___

    A. sharing   B. inter-library loan
    C. inter-library cooperation   D. networking
    E. inter-library transmission

49. The MAIN purpose of library reference service is to   49.___

    A. do research   B. answer patron's questions
    C. arrange special programs   D. write book reviews
    E. maintain order in the library

50. Charging out materials from the library *usually* occurs at the   50.___

    A. reference desk   B. front door
    C. circulation desk   D. A-V department
    E. library director's desk

KEY (CORRECT ANSWERS)

1. B	11. B	21. C	31. D	41. B
2. C	12. D	22. E	32. C	42. C
3. C	13. B	23. B	33. B	43. D
4. A	14. B	24. D	34. A	44. B
5. D	15. C	25. B	35. C	45. D
6. C	16. C	26. B	36. E	46. A
7. C	17. C	27. D	37. C	47. B
8. C	18. E	28. E	38. D	48. B
9. E	19. C	29. C	39. A	49. B
10. C	20. D	30. C	40. E	50. C

EXAMINATION SECTION
TEST 1

DIRECTIONS: Each question or incomplete statement is followed by several suggested answers or completions. Select the one that BEST answers the question or completes the statement. *PRINT THE LETTER OF THE CORRECT ANSWER IN THE SPACE AT THE RIGHT.*

1. Reference materials refer to those materials that   1.____

   A. circulate
   B. are available for inter-library loan
   C. remain in the library
   D. are strictly for the use of the library staff
   E. are used for professional development

2. The process of identifying a work is USUALLY referred to as   2.____

   A. descriptive cataloging   B. accessioning
   C. labeling   D. serializing
   E. marketing

3. The *two most widely used* standard lists of subject headings are: 3.____

   A. Sears List of Subject Headings and ALA Rules
   B. Library of Congress Subject Headings and Sears List of Subject Headings
   C. Dewey and Sears List of Subject Headings
   D. Library of Congress Subject Headings and Dewey
   E. Sears List of Subject Headings and Haykin"s Practical Guide to Subject Headings

4. An example of a book catalog is   4.____

   A. C.B.I.
   B. Sears List of Subject Headings
   C. Library of Congress Catalog
   D. National Union Catalog
   E. Anglo-American Cataloging Rules

5. The Dewey Decimal Classification was developed in 1873 by   5.____

   A. the Library of Congress   B. John Dewey
   C. Melvil Dewey   D. Samuel Dewey
   E. Thomas E. Dewey

6. The Dewey Decimal Classification is composed of _____ main classes.   6.____

   A. 100   B. 2   C. 50   D. 1000   E. 10

7. The Dewey Decimal Classification number *never* has more than _____ to the left.   7.____

   A. 1 digit   B. 2 digits   C. 3 digits
   D. 4 digits   E. 5 digits

8. To distinguish among books assigned the same classification number, another number is   8.____
   assigned. This is called a _____ number.

   A. L.C.   B. N.U.C.   C. title   D. cutter   E. call

9. The classification number and the author number *together* make up the _____ number.   9.__

    A. title   B. cutter   C. L.C.   D. call   E. Dewey

10. The *second most frequently used* classification system in the United States is   10.__

    A. Dewey Decimal Classification
    B. National Union Cata.log
    C. Nelinet Classification
    D. Library of Congress Classification
    E. Sears Classification

11. Reference tools that list books and other materials are called   11.__

    A. encyclopedias   B. compendiums   C. bibliographies
    D. directories   E. almanacs

12. Books that list names of persons or organizations along with pertinent information about them are called   12.__

    A. almanacs   B. encyclopedias of organizations
    C. gazetteers   D. statistical abstracts
    E. directories

13. A collection of maps is referred to as a(n)   13.__

    A. series   B. survey   C. guidebook
    D. atlas   E. gazetteer

14. Descriptive information about cities and countries is usually found in   14.__

    A. atlases   B. guidebooks   C. almanacs
    D. periodicals   E. card catalogs

15. Eric Partridge and Harold Wentworth are *best* known for   15.__

    A. desk encyclopedias   B. unabridged dictionaries
    C. historical dictionaries   D. dictionaries of slang
    E. synonyms and antonyms

16. Evans and Fowler are *best* known for   16.__

    A. dictionaries of current usage   B. historical dictionaries
    C. bibliographies   D. abridged dictionaries
    E. synonyms and antonyms

17. Murray and Craigie are *best* known for   17.__

    A. synonyms and antonyms   B. almanacs
    C. bibliographies   D. dictionaries of current usage
    E. historical dictionaries

18. Funk and Wagnalls, Random House, and Webster's are *best* known for   18.__

    A. historical dictionaries   B. unabridged dictionaries
    C. almanacs   D. abbreviations
    E. bibliographies

19. A comprehensive adult encyclopedia with somewhat less coverage and detail than the Americana or Britannica is   19._____

    A. Whitaker's   B. World Almanac   C. Columbia
    D. World Book   E. Collier's

20. A one-volume general encyclopedia with concise information on a wide range of subjects is   20._____

    A. Encyclopedia Americana   B. World Book Encyclopedia
    C. Columbia Encyclopedia   D. Whitaker's Encyclopedia
    E. Collier's Encyclopedia

21. A popular juvenile encyclopedia is   21._____

    A. Encyclopedia Britannica   B. Americana
    C. Columbia   D. Collier's
    E. World Book

22. Bartlett and Stevenson are *best* known for   22._____

    A. almanacs
    B. directories
    C. handbooks of coins and stamps
    D. handbooks of quotations
    E. handbooks of occupations

23. A standard handbook on parliamentary procedure was authored by   23._____

    A. Smith   B. Robert   C. Carter   D. Jones   E. Wright

24. The sheets of a book, sometimes unsewn, issued in advance of publication for review or promotion purposes, are usually referred to as _____ sheets.   24._____

    A. courtesy   B. advance   C. preview
    D. forward   E. lead

25. In the United States the medal for the *best* picture book of the year is called the _____ medal.   25._____

    A. Illustrator's   B. Caldecott   C. Newbery
    D. Bowker   E. ALA

26. An award presented annually to the author of the MOST distinguished contribution to American literature for children is called the _____ medal.   26._____

    A. Caldecott   B. Illustrator's   C. Newbery
    D. Bowker   E. ALA

27. A microfilm reader which can also be used to make enlargements automatically is called a   27._____

    A. xerox machine   B. reader-writer   C. duplicator
    D. reader-printer   E. printer-reader

28. A character, originally in the form of picture-writing engraved in stone by the ancient Egyptians to convey thoughts or information, is called   28._____

    A. hierophant   B. hierograph   C. hieroglyph
    D. hieratic   E. hierodule

29. The science of control and communication processes in animals and machines is referred to as

    A. interjection   B. interpolation   C. instrumentation
    D. cybernetics   E. symbiosis

29.___

30. The bookbinding process which gives the book a convex spine is called

    A. spining   B. rounding   C. routing
    D. forming   E. smoothing

30.___

31. A novel in which one or more characters are based on real people but are given fictitious names is often referred to as a

    A. biograph   B. roman à clef   C. Gothic novel
    D. petit roman   E. roman du roi

31.___

32. An award presented for originality shown in devising new and improved methods in library technology is called the _____ medal.

    A. Robinson   B. Caldecott   C. Newbery
    D. ALA   E. Roberts

32.___

33. The classification of books relative to their positions on shelves is usually referred to as _____ classification.

    A. bibliographic   B. Sears   C. Dewey
    D. Library of Congress   E. rigid

33.___

34. Another common name for a memorial volume is

    A. festschrift   B. memoirs   C. special edition
    D. limited edition   E. tome

34.___

35. A computerized service developed by the National Library of Medicine in 1971 for rapid bibliographic searching of current medical literature is called

    A. Medfacts   B. Medservice   C. Medlam
    D. Medline   E. Medfast

35.___

36. A work that has been abridged or summarized from some larger work is usually referred to as a(an)

    A. epithet   B. epitome   C. entropy
    D. adaptation   E. adoption

36.___

37. ERIC is an acronym for

    A. Educational Research Instruction Center
    B. Educational Resources Informing Center
    C. Educational Resources Information Center
    D. Educational Resources Instruction Center
    E. Educational Research Incentive Center

37.___

38. The attributing of false names to authors of books is called   38._____

    A. plagiarism   B. pseudepigraph   C. pronephros
    D. pseudomorphism   E. preconization

39. A geographical dictionary is usually called a(n)   39._____

    A. Michelin guide   B. travel guide   C. atlas
    D. guidebook   E. gazetteer

40. Dictionaries devoted to specialized fields, occupations, or professions are generally   40._____
referred to as _____ dictionaries.

    A. encyclopedia   B. usage   C. subject
    D. multi-purpose   E. special

41. A manuscript in book form is called a   41._____

    A. code   B. codex   C. codicil
    D. chrestomathy   E. coda

42. The inscription, used especially in the 15th and 16th centuries, which the printer placed   42._____
at the end of a manuscript or book with facts about its production, author, date, title, etc.,
is called a(n)

    A. colophon   B. summit   C. collating mark
    D. stamp   E. emblem

43. An alphabetical index of words showing the places in the text of a book where each may   43._____
be found is called a

    A. configuration   B. colporteur
    C. continuation order   D. concordance
    E. conversion

44. Copies of a newly published book placed in specificed libraries are designated as   44._____
_____ copies.

    A. assigned   B. deposit   C. reference
    D. honor   E. circulating

45. Material of transitory interest or value is usually referred to as   45._____

    A. ephemeral   B. epicene   C. ephoral
    D. epicurean   E. epicyclic

46. Errors discovered in a book after printing are usually called   46._____

    A. eccentrics   B. espials   C. escheats
    D. eschewals   E. errata

47. The Latin phrase "ex *libris*" designates the   47._____

    A. author   B. title   C. publisher
    D. library   E. distributor

48. A reprint edition of several works of an author is called a(n)   48._____

    A. omnibus book   B. festschrift   C. memorial edition
    D. limited edition   E. special edition

49. A separate printing or reprint of an article or chapter which has appeared first in a maga-   49.___
zine or some other larger work is usually called a(n)

    A. special edition   B. offprint   C. limited edition
    D. processed copy   E. detached copy

50. In a card catalog or index, the entry under which full information is given is called the   50.___

    A. secondary entry   B. collation   C. prime entry
    D. main entry   E. tracing

KEY (CORRECT ANSWERS)

1.	C	11.	C	21.	E	31.	B	41.	B
2.	A	12.	E	22.	D	32.	A	42.	A
3.	B	13.	D	23.	B	33.	E	43.	D
4.	D	14.	B	24.	B	34.	A	44.	B
5.	C	15.	D	25.	B	35.	D	45.	A
6.	E	16.	A	26.	C	36.	B	46.	E
7.	C	17.	E	27.	D	37.	C	47.	D
8.	D	18.	B	28.	C	38.	B	48.	A
9.	D	19.	E	29.	D	39.	E	49.	B
10.	D	20.	C	30.	B	40.	C	50.	D

EXAMINATION SECTION
TEST 1

DIRECTIONS: Each question or incomplete statement is followed by several suggested answers or completions. Select the one that BEST answers the question or completes the statement. *PRINT THE LETTER OF THE CORRECT ANSWER IN THE SPACE AT THE RIGHT.*

1. The BEST known encyclopedia in the Western world, first published in the 18th century, is

    A. WORLD BOOK ENCYCLOPEDIA
    B. COMPTON'S PICTURED ENCYCLOPEDIA
    C. ENCYCLOPEDIA BRITANNICA
    D. ENCYCLOPEDIA AMERICANA

1._____

2. Authority-control records are important in an online catalog environment because they

    A. help prevent *blind* cross-references
    B. expand the capacity of the database
    C. keep the system from overloading
    D. provide access to fugitive materials

2._____

3. The NEW ENCYCLOPEDIA BRITANNICA does NOT include the

    A. Micropaedia
    C. Macropaedia
    B. Monopaedia
    D. Propaedia

3._____

4. Which of the following is NOT the name of an online catalog?

    A. Geobase   B. Dynix   C. Geac   D. OCLC

4._____

5. Nom de plume is synonymous with

    A. pseudonym
    C. given name
    B. nickname
    D. telonism

5._____

6. Component-word searching is another way of saying _____ searching.

    A. key-word
    C. subject
    B. permuterm
    D. author/title

6._____

7. The ENCYCLOPEDIA AMERICANA is ESPECIALLY useful for

    A. finding information about movie stars
    B. finding little-known material about the United States
    C. finding tide charts
    D. doing comprehensive world research

7._____

8. The citation indexes (SCIENCE CITATION INDEX, etc.) are unique in that they

    A. allow searching by the name of an institution
    B. provide access to foreign language journals
    C. allow searching of an author's references
    D. contain millions of unique records

8._____

9. The following are all children's and young adults' encyclopedias EXCEPT   9.__

    A. MERIT STUDENTS ENCYCLOPEDIA
    B. WORLD BOOK ENCYCLOPEDIA
    C. COMPTON'S ENCYCLOPEDIA AND FACT BOOK
    D. COLLIER'S ENCYCLOPEDIA

10. A good online public access catalog (OPAC) can be expected to provide all of the follow-   10.__
ing EXCEPT

    A. author and title access to books and audio-visual materials
    B. the loan status of materials that circulate
    C. information regarding who a book has been loaned to
    D. the place and publisher of each book in the catalog

11. Of the points to consider in a systematic evaluation of an encyclopedia, the LEAST   11.__
important one is

    A. cost   B. viewpoint and objectivity
    C. subject coverage   D. number of pages

12. Widespread searching of bibliographic databases dates back to   12.__

    A. the 1950's   B. 1960
    C. the mid-1980's   D. the early 1970's

13. The format of a reference set means the   13.__

    A. writing style
    B. binding and size
    C. authority of contributors
    D. viewpoint and objectivity

14. The FIRST bibliographic databases were by-products of   14.__

    A. progress in NASA technology
    B. online card catalogs such as OCLC
    C. information dissemination centers
    D. the computerized typesetting operation

15. A patron asks your advice as a librarian on a set of encyclopedias he is considering for   15.__
his family.
The MOST helpful response for you is to

    A. give limited advice and provide the patron with professional reviews of the set
       under question
    B. give no advice for fear of repercussions from sales-persons and publishers
    C. endorse or condemn the set whole-heartedly, depending on your own opinion
    D. refer the patron to the director of the library

16. The four basic components of the online industry include all of the following EXCEPT   16.__

    A. libraries and information centers
    B. library school administrators
    C. end-users who request information
    D. database producers

17. McGraw-Hill's ENCYCLOPEDIA OF WORLD ART is an example of a _____ encyclopedia.   17._____

    A. children's   B. subject
    C. supermarket   D. foreign

18. Which of the following bibliographic databases is NOT produced by a federal government   18._____
    agency or federally-supported institution?

    A. ERIC   B. COMPENDEX   C. AGRICOLA   D. MEDLINE

19. A ready-reference work is one which   19._____

    A. is allowed to circulate outside of the library
    B. is especially difficult to use
    C. arrives on a monthly basis
    D. is useful for *quick* questions of a factual nature

20. All of the following are examples of source documents EXCEPT   20._____

    A. patents   B. conference papers
    C. indexes   D. newspapers

21. The STATISTICAL ABSTRACT OF THE UNITED STATES is a compendium in the sense   21._____
    that it

    A. contains statistics on a wide range of subjects
    B. is published on an annual basis
    C. is a summary of U.S. Census data
    D. can be used for research in education

22. The number EJ121478, as part of an ERIC record, would indicate that the material refer-   22._____
    enced

    A. is a journal article
    B. is a book
    C. is an ERIC document on microfiche
    D. was entered in the database in 1978

23. Which of the following almanacs is published in London, England?   23._____

    A. WHITAKER'S ALMANAC
    B. INFORMATION PLEASE ALMANAC
    C. WORLD ALMANAC AND BOOK OF FACTS
    D. THE PEOPLE'S ALMANAC

24. A thesaurus which accompanies an index such as ERIC is a list of   24._____

    A. corporate authors   B. journals indexed
    C. stop words   D. assigned descriptors

25. Ready-reference materials include all of the following EXCEPT   25._____

    A. STATISTICAL ABSTRACT OF THE UNITED STATES
    B. INFORMATION PLEASE ALMANAC
    C. BIOLOGICAL ABSTRACTS
    D. THE NEW YORK RED BOOK

KEY (CORRECT ANSWERS)

1. C	11. D
2. A	12. D
3. B	13. B
4. A	14. D
5. A	15. A
6. A	16. B
7. B	17. B
8. C	18. B
9. D	19. D
10. C	20. C

21. C
22. A
23. A
24. D
25. C

————

TEST 2

DIRECTIONS: Each question or incomplete statement is followed by several suggested answers or completions. Select the one that BEST answers the question or completes the statement. *PRINT THE LETTER OF THE CORRECT ANSWER IN THE SPACE AT THE RIGHT.*

1. The U.S. National Library of Medicine produces all of the following databases EXCEPT   1._____

    A. EMBASE   B. AIDSLINE   C. CANCERLIT   D. MEDLINE

2. H.W. Wilson's CURRENT BIOGRAPHY provides   2._____

    A. essay-length biographical information
    B. reference to information in BIOGRAPHY INDEX
    C. no more information on an individual than is provided by WHO'S WHO
    D. reviews of best-selling biographies

3. The database which provides access to fugitive materials in education is   3._____

    A. Academic Index
    B. Education Index
    C. ERIC
    D. Mental Measurements Yearbook

4. All of the following are covered in CONTEMPORARY AUTHORS EXCEPT   4._____

    A. screenwriters   B. poets
    C. dramatists   D. technical writers

5. Boolean logic utilizes all of the following logical operators EXCEPT   5._____

    A. if   B. or   C. not   D. and

6. A prescriptive dictionary is one which   6._____

    A. discusses in great detail the origin of a word
    B. adheres to tradition and historical authority for word definitions and approved usage
    C. attempts to relate every possible definition and usage of a word
    D. is published only in the United States

7. Free-text searching in a bibliographic database means   7._____

    A. searching several descriptors at one time
    B. using Boolean logic in your search
    C. searching without the use of controlled vocabulary
    D. searching only titles and abstracts

8. ABRIDGED INDEX MEDICUS differs from INDEX MEDICUS in that it   8._____

    A. contains citations to English-language journals only
    B. contains only information from the last twelve months
    C. contains citations to foreign-language journals only
    D. is not published by the National Library of Medicine

9. The two PRINCIPAL operations of public services are   9.__
   A. circulation and reference
   B. reference and serials management
   C. circulation and collection development
   D. reference and classification

10. Of the following reasons for an academic library to acquire the DICTIONARY OF AMER-   10.__
    ICAN SLANG, which is the LEAST valid?

    A. Most regular dictionaries do not indicate the variations of meaning of given slang
       terms or words.
    B. Students often come across expressions which are not defined well in ordinary dic-
       tionaries.
    C. It is a good source to check on the language used by an author to convey a charac-
       ter's background or social class.
    D. Students and librarians alike enjoy reading through it during their leisure time.

11. Collection maintenance includes all of the following EXCEPT   11.__
    A. taking inventory   B. reshelving books
    C. identifying overdues   D. shelf-reading

12. A gazetteer is a   12.__

    A. biographical dictionary
    B. good source for looking up phases of the moon
    C. geographical dictionary
    D. guide to motels throughout the United States

13. A Dewey Decimal Classification number never has MORE than how many digits to the   13.__
    LEFT of the decimal?

    A. Four   B. Five   C. Three   D. Two

14. In MOST government depository libraries, the government documents are arranged on   14.__
    the shelves

    A. by Superintendent of Documents numbers
    B. by Library of Congress call numbers
    C. by Dewey Decimal numbers
    D. alphabetically by title

15. The Library of Congress Classification System is different from the Dewey Decimal Clas- 15.__
    sification System in that it

    A. arranges books on the shelf by subject
    B. does not include author numbers
    C. is not frequently used by libraries in the United States
    D. was developed to meet the needs of a specific library's collection

16. The BEST reference source for finding, in detail, the organization and activities of all U.S. government agencies is

    A. POLITICS IN AMERICA
    B. THE STATESMAN'S YEARBOOK
    C. UNITED STATES GOVERNMENT MANUAL
    D. MOODY'S MUNICIPAL AND GOVERNMENT MANUAL

16.____

17. The added entries in a catalog record could be for

    A. joint authors, titles, or series
    B. joint authors, series, or subjects
    C. joint authors, titles, or subjects
    D. titles, publishers, or series

17.____

18. Which of the following illustrates a directional question?

    A. How far is Syracuse from Lake Ontario?
    B. Where is the public telephone?
    C. Where can I find a biographical dictionary of presidents?
    D. Is Italy to the east of Spain?

18.____

19. You are performing an online bibliographic search for a patron and have brought up a set consisting of 300 records.
    Of the following, which is the LEAST valid way of limiting the search in order to avoid printing such a large set?

    A. Limit the search to a certain range of years
    B. Redefine the search using more specific descriptors
    C. Print only the first 40 records of the set
    D. Cut out references to articles in languages the patron cannot read

19.____

20. All of the following are examples of primary sources EXCEPT

    A. diaries   B. biographies
    C. letters   D. memoirs

20.____

21. *What is the population of Mexico City?* would MOST likely be classified as what type of reference question?

    A. Ready reference   B. Directional
    C. Research on a topic   D. Instructional

21.____

22. Something you would NOT expect to find in a vertical file is

    A. a monograph   B. a pamphlet
    C. a folded map   D. newspaper clippings

22.____

23. Logical product, logical sum, and logical difference are all part of what type of searching?

    A. Permuterm logic   B. Keyword-in-context (KWIC)
    C. Statistical logic   D. Boolean logic

23.____

24. Keyword-in-context (KWIC) indexing is also called _____ indexing.

    A. title   B. comprehensive
    C. subject   D. permutation

24.____

25. The MARC format was developed at the

    A. National Library of Medicine
    B. British Library
    C. Library of Congress
    D. Smithsonian Institute

25.__

26. Patrons of a general library are usually MOST aware of which of the following library activities?

    A. Circulation   B. Accession
    C. Cataloging   D. Reference

26.__

27. Three of the following four are consequences of the copy-righting of books by the U.S. government.
Which is NOT such a consequence?

    A. Protecting author's rights
    B. Encouraging writing
    C. Securing deposit material for the government
    D. Government endorsement of the copyrighted texts

27.__

28. The term *cataloging in publication* refers to a cataloging program under which cataloging information

    A. appears in the PUBLISHERS' WEEKLY
    B. appears in the National Union Catalog
    C. appears in the publication itself
    D. is prepared by the publisher

28.__

29. The MAJOR use of a formal statement of a library's objective is

    A. serving as a guideline for program development and services
    B. justifying library staffing to the board and public
    C. convincing the governing body of the need for financial support
    D. training library staff in improved methods and practices

29.__

30. Circulation statistics should be gathered PRIMARILY for the purpose of

    A. justifying the library budget
    B. improving library service
    C. cutting library costs
    D. analyzing personnel performance

30.__

KEY (CORRECT ANSWERS)

1.	A	16.	C
2.	A	17.	A
3.	C	18.	B
4.	D	19.	C
5.	A	20.	B
6.	B	21.	A
7.	C	22.	A
8.	A	23.	D
9.	A	24.	D
10.	D	25.	C
11.	C	26.	A
12.	C	27.	D
13.	C	28.	C
14.	A	29.	A
15.	D	30.	B

———————

TEST 3

DIRECTIONS: Each question or incomplete statement is followed by several suggested answers or completions. Select the one that BEST answers the question or completes the statement. *PRINT THE LETTER OF THE CORRECT ANSWER IN THE SPACE AT THE RIGHT.*

1. A typical reference in the READER'S GUIDE TO PERIODICAL LITERATURE would include all of the following EXCEPT

    A. author   B. title of the article
    C. journal name   D. journal abstract

    1.__

2. An example of a subject authority list used in cataloging is the

    A. THESAURUS OF ERIC DESCRIPTORS
    B. LIBRARY OF CONGRESS SUBJECT HEADINGS
    C. NEW YORK TIMES INDEX
    D. CINAHL SUBJECT HEADING LIST

    2.__

3. An example of a nonperiodical serial is

    A. EUROPA YEARBOOK
    B. AQUACULTURE MAGAZINE
    C. THE WASHINGTON POST
    D. JOURNAL OF THE AMERICAN MEDICAL ASSOCIATION

    3.__

4. The Superintendent of Documents classification system arranges government documents on the shelves

    A. alphabetically by title
    B. by government agency
    C. alphabetically by author
    D. according to date of printing

    4.__

5. Which of the following is an example of an open-ended question?

    A. Would you like books or magazine articles?
    B. You say you need to know the elevation of Denver?
    C. What kind of information about sharks are you looking for?
    D. Have you ever used our online catalog?

    5.__

6. Scientific Information's weekly CURRENT CONTENTS consists of

    A. reproductions of journal contents pages
    B. a subject index for scientific journals
    C. author and title indexes for current periodicals
    D. scientific journal abstracts

    6.__

7. All of the following are bibliographic utilities involved in resource sharing EXCEPT

    A. OCLC   B. RLIN   C. DYNIX   D. UTLAS

    7.__

8. The MAIN objective of reference negotiation is to   8._____

    A. save the librarian's time
    B. steer patrons away from heavily used sources
    C. find out what the patron specifically needs
    D. instruct patrons in the proper use of reference materials

9. Which of the following PROPERLY demonstrates a logical product and logical difference   9._____
search statement?

    A. Dogs and cats, not birds
    B. (Dogs or cats) and not birds
    C. Dogs and not birds or cats
    D. Dogs and (cats or birds)

10. The generally accepted definition of a serial includes all of the following EXCEPT   10._____

    A. yearbooks   B. newspapers
    C. theses   D. journals

11. ESSAY AND GENERAL LITERATURE INDEX is MOST useful for locating   11._____

    A. a specific chapter of a book
    B. magazine and journal articles
    C. biographical essays
    D. a pamphlet or newsletter

12. What do LIBRARY JOURNAL, SHEEHY'S GUIDE TO REFERENCE BOOKS, and   12._____
ARBA have in common?
They

    A. are all periodicals
    B. discuss management of online catalogs
    C. provide critical evaluation of reference materials
    D. discuss only highly recommended reference sources

13. SHORT STORY INDEX covers stories published   13._____

    A. on all subjects except science fiction
    B. in collections and the NEW YORK TIMES
    C. in collections and periodicals
    D. by American authors only

14. One way in which nonperiodical serials (such as yearbooks) are different from periodical   14._____
serials (such as journals) is that nonperiodicals are

    A. published several times a year
    B. usually a collection of articles
    C. usually ordered by subscription
    D. usually acquired through a standing order

15. Of the general serial sources listed below, which is the only one that includes newspa-   15.__
pers?

    A. STANDARD PERIODICAL DIRECTORY
    B. GALE DIRECTORY OF PUBLICATIONS
    C. ULRICH'S INTERNATIONAL PERIODICALS DIRECTORY
    D. IRREGULAR SERIALS AND ANNUALS

16. The READER'S GUIDE TO PERIODICAL LITERATURE indexes   16.__

    A. magazines and newspapers
    B. popular magazines
    C. scholarly journals
    D. short story anthologies

17. Ethnic numbers are added to classification symbols so as to arrange books by   17.__

    A. subject   B. place of printing
    C. author   D. language

18. End-matter items could include all of the following EXCEPT   18.__

    A. appendices   B. bibliographies
    C. tables of contents   D. indexes

19. Which of the following BEST describes a jobber?   19.__
A

    A. company which produces databases
    B. corporate body responsible for placing a book on the market
    C. wholesale bookseller who stocks books and supplies them to libraries
    D. person skilled in writing computer programs

20. The word *an* is a stopword on the Medline database.   20.__
This means that

    A. it cannot be used as a search term in the database
    B. Medline includes articles such as *an* and *the* when alphabetizing by title
    C. if you type in that word, you will exit the database
    D. you cannot use Medline when searching for a title that begins with *an*

21. Of the following queries, which could NOT be answered by consulting a regular dictio-   21.__
nary?

    A. What is the Golden Rule?
    B. How deep is a fathom?
    C. Does "humble" come from the same root as "human"?
    D. What are the rules for writing a sonnet?

22. An accurate definition of annals would be a(n)   22.__

    A. serial publication issued once a year
    B. anonymous publication
    C. record of events arranged in chronological order
    D. bibliography of an author's writings arranged by date of publication

23. West's FEDERAL PRACTICE DIGEST is an index to   23.____

  A. United States Supreme Court cases
  B. United States statutes
  C. New York State statutes
  D. The Code of Federal Regulations

24. MOST federal government documents are printed by   24.____

  A. the Government Printing Office
  B. the Library of Congress
  C. the United States Printing Office
  D. Congress

25. Setting aside a separate section for oversized books is an example of   25.____

  A. subject cataloging
  B. parallel arrangement
  C. a special materials collection
  D. Dewey Decimal Classification

KEY (CORRECT ANSWERS)

1.	D	11.	A
2.	B	12.	C
3.	A	13.	C
4.	B	14.	D
5.	C	15.	B
6.	A	16.	B
7.	C	17.	D
8.	C	18.	C
9.	A	19.	C
10.	C	20.	A

21.	D
22.	C
23.	A
24.	A
25.	B

EXAMINATION SECTION
TEST 1

DIRECTIONS: Each question or incomplete statement is followed by several suggested answers or completions. Select the one that BEST answers the question or completes the statement. *PRINT THE LETTER OF THE CORRECT ANSWER IN THE SPACE AT THE RIGHT.*

1. When conducting a needs assessment for the purpose of education planning, an agency's FIRST step is to identify or provide

    A. a profile of population characteristics
    B. barriers to participation
    C. existing resources
    D. profiles of competing resources

1.____

2. Research has demonstrated that of the following, the most effective medium for communicating with external publics is/are

    A. video news releases
    B. television
    C. radio
    D. newspapers

2.____

3. Basic ideas behind the effort to influence the attitudes and behaviors of a constituency include each of the following, EXCEPT the idea that

    A. words, rather than actions or events, are most likely to motivate
    B. demands for action are a usual response
    C. self-interest usually figures heavily into public involvement
    D. the reliability of change programs is difficult to assess

3.____

4. An agency representative is trying to craft a pithy message to constituents in order to encourage the use of agency program resources. Choosing an audience for such messages is easiest when the message

    A. is project- or behavior-based
    B. is combined with other messages
    C. is abstract
    D. has a broad appeal

4.____

5. Of the following factors, the most important to the success of an agency's external education or communication programs is the

    A. amount of resources used to implement them
    B. public's prior experiences with the agency
    C. real value of the program to the public
    D. commitment of the internal audience

5.____

6. A representative for a state agency is being interviewed by a reporter from a local news network. The representative is being asked to defend a program that is extremely unpopular in certain parts of the municipality. When a constituency is known to be opposed to a position, the most useful communication strategy is to present

6.____

    A. only the arguments that are consistent with constituents' views
    B. only the agency's side of the issue
    C. both sides of the argument as clearly as possible
    D. both sides of the argument, omitting key information about the opposing position

7. The most significant barriers to effective agency community relations include   7.___
      I. widespread distrust of communication strategies
      II. the media's "watchdog" stance
      III. public apathy
      IV. statutory opposition

    A. I only
    B. I and II
    C. II and III
    D. III and IV

8. In conducting an education program, many agencies use workshops and seminars in a   8.___
classroom setting. Advantages of classroom-style teaching over other means of educating the public include each of the following, EXCEPT:

    A. enabling an instructor to verify learning through testing and interaction with the target audience
    B. enabling hands-on practice and other participatory learning techniques
    C. ability to reach an unlimited number of participants in a given length of time
    D. ability to convey the latest, most up-to-date information

9. The _____ model of community relations is characterized by an attempt to persuade   9.___
the public to adopt the agency's point of view.

    A. two-way symmetric
    B. two-way asymmetric
    C. public information
    D. press agency/publicity

10. Important elements of an internal situation analysis include the   10.___
      I. list of agency opponents
      II. communication audit
      III. updated organizational almanac
      IV. stakeholder analysis

    A. I and II
    B. I, II and III
    C. II and III
    D. I, II, III and IV

11. Government agency information efforts typically involve each of the following objectives,   11.___
EXCEPT to

    A. implement changes in the policies of government agencies to align with public opinion
    B. communicate the work of agencies
    C. explain agency techniques in a way that invites input from citizens
    D. provide citizen feedback to government administrators

12. Factors that are likely to influence the effectiveness of an educational campaign include the

      I.   level of homogeneity among intended participants
     II.   number and types of media used
   III.   receptivity of the intended participants
   IV.   level of specificity in the message or behavior to be taught

   A.   I and II
   B.   I, II and III
   C.   II and III
   D.   I, II, III and IV

12.____

13. An agency representative is writing instructional objectives that will later help to measure the effectiveness of an educational program. Which of the following verbs, included in an objective, would be MOST helpful for the purpose of measuring effectiveness?

   A.   Know
   B.   Identify
   C.   Learn
   D.   Comprehend

13.____

14. A state education agency wants to encourage participation in a program that has just received a boost through new federal legislation. The program is intended to include participants from a wide variety of socioeconomic and other demographic characteristics. The agency wants to launch a broad-based program that will inform virtually every interested party in the state about the program's new circumstances. In attempting to deliver this message to such a wide-ranging constituency, the agency's best practice would be to

   A.   broadcast the same message through as many different media channels as possible
   B.   focus on one discrete segment of the public at a time
   C.   craft a message whose appeal is as broad as the public itself
   D.   let the program's achievements speak for themselves and rely on word-of-mouth

14.____

15. Advantages associated with using the World Wide Web as an educational tool include

      I.   an appeal to younger generations of the public
     II.   visually-oriented, interactive learning
   III.   learning that is not confined by space, time, or institutional association
   IV.   a variety of methods for verifying use and learning

   A.   I only
   B.   I and II
   C.   I, II and III
   D.   I, II, III and IV

15.____

16. In agencies involved in health care, community relations is a critical function because it

   A.   serves as an intermediary between the agency and consumers
   B.   generates a clear mission statement for agency goals and priorities
   C.   ensures patient privacy while satisfying the media's right to information
   D.   helps marketing professionals determine the wants and needs of agency constituents

16.____

17. After an extensive campaign to promote its newest program to constituents, an agency learns that most of the audience did not understand the intended message. Most likely, the agency has

    A. chosen words that were intended to inform, rather than persuade
    B. not accurately interpreted what the audience really needed to know
    C. overestimated the ability of the audience to receive and process the message
    D. compensated for noise that may have interrupted the message

17.___

18. The necessary elements that lead to conviction and motivation in the minds of participants in an educational or information program include each of the following, EXCEPT the _____ of the message.

    A. acceptability
    B. intensity
    C. single-channel appeal
    D. pervasiveness

18.___

19. Printed materials are often at the core of educational programs provided by public agencies. The primary disadvantage associated with print is that it

    A. does not enable comprehensive treatment of a topic
    B. is generally unreliable in term of assessing results
    C. is often the most expensive medium available
    D. is constrained by time

19.___

20. Traditional thinking on public opinion holds that there is about _____ percent of the public who are pivotal to shifting the balance and momentum of opinion—they are concerned about an issue, but not fanatical, and interested enough to pay attention to a reasoned discussion.

    A. 2
    B. 10
    C. 33
    D. 51

20.___

21. One of the most useful guidelines for influencing attitude change among people is to

    A. invite the target audience to come to you, rather than approaching them
    B. use moral appeals as the primary approach
    C. use concrete images to enable people to see the results of behaviors or indifference
    D. offer tangible rewards to people for changes in behaviors

21.___

22. An agency is attempting to evaluate the effectiveness of its educational program. For this purpose, it wants to observe several focus groups discussing the same program. Which of the following would NOT be a guideline for the use of focus groups?

    A. Focus groups should only include those who have participated in the program.
    B. Be sure to accurately record the discussion.
    C. The same questions should be asked at each focus group meeting.
    D. It is often helpful to have a neutral, non-agency employee facilitate discussions.

22.___

23. Research consistently shows that _____ is the determinant most likely to make a newspaper editor run a news release.

    A. novelty
    B. prominence
    C. proximity
    D. conflict

23.____

24. Which of the following is NOT one of the major variables to take into account when considering a population-needs assessment?

    A. State of program development
    B. Resources available
    C. Demographics
    D. Community attitudes

24.____

25. The first step in any communications audit is to

    A. develop a research instrument
    B. determine how the organization currently communicates
    C. hire a contractor
    D. determine which audience to assess

25.____

KEY (CORRECT ANSWERS)

1. A		11. A
2. D		12. D
3. A		13. B
4. A		14. B
5. D		15. C
6. C		16. A
7. D		17. B
8. C		18. C
9. B		19. B
10. C		20. B

21. C
22. A
23. C
24. C
25. D

TEST 2

DIRECTIONS: Each question or incomplete statement is followed by several suggested answers or completions. Select the one that BEST answers the question or completes the statement. *PRINT THE LETTER OF THE CORRECT ANSWER IN THE SPACE AT THE RIGHT.*

1. A public relations practitioner at an agency has just composed a press release highlight-   1._
    ing a program's recent accomplishments and success stories. In pitching such releases
    to print outlets, the practitioner should
    I.   e-mail, mail, or send them by messenger
    II.   address them to "editor" or "news director"
    III. have an assistant call all media contacts by telephone
    IV.   ask reporters or editors how they prefer to receive them

    A. I and II   B. I and IV   C. II, III and IV   D. III only

2. The "output goals" of an educational program are MOST likely to include   2._

    A. specified ratings of services by participants on a standardized scale
    B. observable effects on a given community or clientele
    C. the number of instructional hours provided
    D. the number of participants served

3. An agency wants to evaluate satisfaction levels among program participants, and mails   3._
    out questionnaires to everyone who has been enrolled in the last year. The primary prob-
    lem associated with this method of evaluative research is that it

    A. poses a significant inconvenience for respondents
    B. is inordinately expensive
    C. does not allow for follow-up or clarification questions
    D. usually involves a low response rate

4. A communications audit is an important tool for measuring   4._

    A. the depth of penetration of a particular message or program
    B. the cost of the organization's information campaigns
    C. how key audiences perceive an organization
    D. the commitment of internal stakeholders

5. The "ABC's" of written learning objectives include each of the following, EXCEPT   5._

    A. Audience   B. Behavior   C. Conditions   D. Delineation

6. When attempting to change the behaviors of constituents, it is important to keep in mind   6._
    that
    I.   most people are skeptical of communications that try to get them to change
          their behaviors
    II.   in most cases, a person selects the media to which he exposes himself
    III. people tend to react defensively to messages or programs that rely on fear
          as a motivating factor
    IV.   programs should aim for the broadest appeal possible in order to include as
          many participants as possible

    A. I and II   B. I, II and III   C. II and III   D. I, II, III and IV

7. The "laws" of public opinion include the idea that it is   7.____

     A. useful for anticipating emergencies
     B. not sensitive to important events
     C. basically determined by self-interest
     D. sustainable through persistent appeals

8. Which of the following types of evaluations is used to measure public attitudes before   8.____
and after an information/educational program?

     A. retrieval study
     B. copy test
     C. quota sampling
     D. benchmark study

9. The primary source for internal communications is/are usually   9.____

     A. flow charts
     B. meetings
     C. voice mail
     D. printed publications

10. An agency representative is putting together informational materials—brochures and a   10.____
newsletter—outlining changes in one of the state's biggest benefits programs. In assembling print materials as a medium for delivering information to the public, the representative should keep in mind each of the following trends:
     I. For various reasons, the reading capabilities of the public are in general decline
     II. Without tables and graphs to help illustrate the changes, it is unlikely that the message will be delivered effectively
     III. Professionals and career-oriented people are highly receptive to information written in the form of a journal article or empirical study
     IV. People tend to be put off by print materials that use itemized and bulleted (•) lists.

     A. I and II   B. I, II and III   C. II and III   D. I, II, III and IV

11. Which of the following steps in a problem-oriented information campaign would typically   11.____
be implemented FIRST?

     A. Deciding on tactics
     B. Determining a communications strategy
     C. Evaluating the problem's impact
     D. Developing an organizational strategy

12. A common pitfall in conducting an educational program is to   12._

    A. aim it at the wrong target audience
    B. overfund it
    C. leave it in the hands of people who are in the business of education, rather than those with expertise in the business of the organization
    D. ignore the possibility that some other organization is meeting the same educational need for the target audience

13. The key factors that affect the credibility of an agency's educational program include   13._

    A. organization
    B. scope
    C. sophistication
    D. penetration

14. Research on public opinion consistently demonstrates that it is   14._

    A. easy to move people toward a strong opinion on anything, as long as they are approached directly through their emotions
    B. easier to move people away from an opinion they currently hold than to have them form an opinion about something they have not previously cared about
    C. easy to move people toward a strong opinion on anything, as long as the message appeals to their reason and intellect
    D. difficult to move people toward a strong opinion on anything, no matter what the approach

15. In conducting an education program, many agencies use meetings and conferences to educate an audience about the organization and its programs. Advantages associated with this approach include   15._
        I. a captive audience that is known to be interested in the topic
        II. ample opportunities for verifying learning
        III. cost-efficient meeting space
        IV. the ability to provide information on a wider variety of subjects

    A. I and II
    B. I, III and IV
    C. II and III
    D. I, II, III and IV

16. An agency is attempting to evaluate the effectiveness of its educational programs. For this purpose, it wants to observe several focus groups discussing particular programs. For this purpose, a focus group should never number more than _____ participants.   16._

    A. 5   B. 10   C. 15   D. 20

17. A _____ speech is written so that several agency members can deliver it to different audiences with only minor variations.   17._

    A. basic   B. printed   C. quota   D. pattern

18. Which of the following statements about public opinion is generally considered to be FALSE?   18.____

    A. Opinion is primarily reactive rather than proactive.
    B. People have more opinions about goals than about the means by which to achieve them.
    C. Facts tend to shift opinion in the accepted direction when opinion is not solidly structured.
    D. Public opinion is based more on information than desire.

19. An agency is trying to promote its educational program. As a general rule, the agency should NOT assume that   19.____

    A. people will only participate if they perceive an individual benefit
    B. promotions need to be aimed at small, discrete groups
    C. if the program is good, the audience will find out about it
    D. a variety of methods, including advertising, special events, and direct mail, should be considered

20. In planning a successful educational program, probably the first and most important question for an agency to ask is: 20.____

    A. What will be the content of the program?
    B. Who will be served by the program?
    C. When is the best time to schedule the program?
    D. Why is the program necessary?

21. Media kits are LEAST likely to contain   21.____

    A. fact sheets
    B. memoranda
    C. photographs with captions
    D. news releases

22. The use of pamphlets and booklets as media for communication with the public often involves the disadvantage that   22.____

    A. the messages contained within them are frequently nonspecific
    B. it is difficult to measure their effectiveness in delivering the message
    C. there are few opportunities for people to refer to them
    D. color reproduction is poor

23. The most important prerequisite of a good educational program is an   23.____

    A. abundance of resources to implement it
    B. individual staff unit formed for the purpose of program delivery
    C. accurate needs assessment
    D. uneducated constituency

24. After an education program has been delivered, an agency conducts a program evalua-   24.___
tion to determine whether its objectives have been met. General rules about how to conduct such an education program evaluation include each of the following, EXCEPT that it

    A.   must be done immediately after the program has been implemented
    B.   should be simple and easy to use
    C.   should be designed so that tabulation of responses can take place quickly and
        inexpensively
    D.   should solicit mostly subjective, open-ended responses if the audience was large

25. Using electronic media such as television as means of educating the public is typically   25.___
recommended ONLY for agencies that
    I.   have a fairly simple message to begin with
    II.   want to reach the masses, rather than a targeted audience
    III.   have substantial financial resources
    IV.   accept that they will not be able to measure the results of the campaign with
        much precision

    A.   I and II
    B.   I, II and III
    C.   II and IV
    D.   I, II, III and IV

KEY (CORRECT ANSWERS)

1.	B		11.	C
2.	C		12.	D
3.	D		13.	A
4.	C		14.	D
5.	D		15.	B
6.	B		16.	B
7.	C		17.	D
8.	D		18.	D
9.	D		19.	C
10.	A		20.	D

21.	B
22.	B
23.	C
24.	D
25.	D

Evaluating Conclusions in Light of Known Facts

EXAMINATION SECTION
TEST 1

DIRECTIONS: Each question or incomplete statement is followed by several suggested answers or completions. Select the one that BEST answers the question or completes the statement. *PRINT THE LETTER OF THE CORRECT ANSWER IN THE SPACE AT THE RIGHT.*

Questions 1-9.

DIRECTIONS: In questions 1-9, you will read a set of facts and a conclusion drawn from them. The conclusion may be valid or invalid, based on the facts—it's your task to determine the validity of the conclusion.

For each question, select the letter before the statement that BEST expresses the relationship between the given facts and the conclusion that has been drawn from them. Your choices are:
A. The facts prove the conclusion
B. The facts disprove the conclusion; or
C. The facts neither prove nor disprove the conclusion.

1. FACTS: If the supervisor retires, James, the assistant supervisor, will not be transferred to another department. James will be promoted to supervisor if he is not transferred. The supervisor retired.

   CONCLUSION: James will be promoted to supervisor.

   A. The facts prove the conclusion.
   B. The facts disprove the conclusion.
   C. The facts neither prove nor disprove the conclusion.

   1._____

2. FACTS: In the town of Luray, every player on the softball team works at Luray National Bank. In addition, every player on the Luray softball team wears glasses.

   CONCLUSION: At least some of the people who work at Luray National Bank wear glasses.

   A. The facts prove the conclusion.
   B. The facts disprove the conclusion.
   C. The facts neither prove nor disprove the conclusion.

   2._____

3. FACTS: The only time Henry and June go out to dinner is on an evening when they have childbirth classes. Their childbirth classes meet on Tuesdays and Thursdays.

   CONCLUSION: Henry and June never go out to dinner on Friday or Saturday.

   A. The facts prove the conclusion.
   B. The facts disprove the conclusion.
   C. The facts neither prove nor disprove the conclusion.

   3._____

4. FACTS: Every player on the field hockey team has at least one bruise. Everyone on the field hockey team also has scarred knees.

   CONCLUSION: Most people with both bruises and scarred knees are field hockey players.

   A. The facts prove the conclusion.
   B. The facts disprove the conclusion.
   C. The facts neither prove nor disprove the conclusion.

   4.__

5. FACTS: In the chess tournament, Lance will win his match against Jane if Jane wins her match against Mathias. If Lance wins his match against Jane, Christine will not win her match against Jane.

   CONCLUSION: Christine will not win her match against Jane if Jane wins her match against Mathias.

   A. The facts prove the conclusion.
   B. The facts disprove the conclusion.
   C. The facts neither prove nor disprove the conclusion.

   5.__

6. FACTS: No green lights on the machine are indicators for the belt drive status. Not all of the lights on the machine's upper panel are green. Some lights on the machine's lower panel are green.

   CONCLUSION: The green lights on the machine's lower panel may be indicators for the belt drive status.

   A. The facts prove the conclusion.
   B. The facts disprove the conclusion.
   C. The facts neither prove nor disprove the conclusion.

   6.__

7. FACTS: At a small, one-room country school, there are eight students: Amy, Ben, Carla, Dan, Elliot, Francine, Greg, and Hannah. Each student is in either the 6th, 7th, or 8th grade. Either two or three students are in each grade. Amy, Dan, and Francine are all in different grades. Ben and Elliot are both in the 7th grade. Hannah and Carl are in the same grade.

   CONCLUSION: Exactly three students are in the 7th grade.

   A. The facts prove the conclusion.
   B. The facts disprove the conclusion.
   C. The facts neither prove nor disprove the conclusion.

   7.__

8. FACTS: Two married couples are having lunch together. Two of the four people are German and two are Russian, but in each couple the nationality of a spouse is not necessarily the same as the other's. One person in the group is a teacher, the other a lawyer, one an engineer, and the other a writer. The teacher is a Russian man. The writer is Russian, and her husband is an engineer. One of the people, Mr. Stern, is German.

   CONCLUSION: Mr. Stern's wife is a writer.

   8.__

A.   The facts prove the conclusion.
B.   The facts disprove the conclusion.
C.   The facts neither prove nor disprove the conclusion.

9.   FACTS: The flume ride at the county fair is open only to children who are at least 36   9.____
     inches tall. Lisa is 30 inches tall. John is shorter than Henry, but more than 10 inches
     taller than Lisa.

     CONCLUSION: Lisa is the only one who can't ride the flume ride.

     A.   The facts prove the conclusion.
     B.   The facts disprove the conclusion.
     C.   The facts neither prove nor disprove the conclusion.

Questions 10-17.

DIRECTIONS: Questions 10-17 are based on the following reading passage. It is not your
              knowledge of the particular topic that is being tested, but your ability to reason
              based on what you have read. The passage is likely to detail several proposed
              courses of action and factors affecting these proposals. The reading passage
              is followed by a conclusion or outcome based on the facts in the passage, or a
              description of a decision taken regarding the situation. The conclusion is fol-
              lowed by a number of statements that have a possible connection to the con-
              clusion. For each statement, you are to determine whether:

              A.   The statement proves the conclusion.
              B.   The statement supports the conclusion but does not prove it.
              C.   The statement disproves the conclusion.
              D.   The statement weakens the conclusion but does not disprove it.
              E.   The statement has no relevance to the conclusion.

Remember that the conclusion after the passage is to be accepted as the outcome of
what actually happened, and that you are being asked to evaluate the impact each statement would have had on the conclusion.

PASSAGE:

The Grand Army of Foreign Wars, a national veteran's organization, is struggling to
maintain its National Home, where the widowed spouses and orphans of deceased members
are housed together in a small village-like community. The Home is open to spouses and children who are bereaved for any reason, regardless of whether the member's death was
related to military service, but a new global conflict has led to a dramatic surge in the number
of members' deaths: many veterans who re-enlisted for the conflict have been killed in action.

The Grand Army of Foreign Wars is considering several options for handling the
increased number of applications for housing at the National Home, which has been traditionally supported by membership dues. At its national convention, it will choose only one of the
following:

The first idea is a one-time $50 tax on all members, above and beyond the dues they pay
already. Since the organization has more than a million members, this tax should be sufficient

for the construction and maintenance of new housing for applicants on the existing grounds of the National Home. The idea is opposed, however, by some older members who live on fixed incomes. These members object in principle to the taxation of Grand Army members. The Grand Army has never imposed a tax on its members.

The second idea is to launch a national fund-raising drive and public relations campaign that will attract donations for the National Home. Several national celebrities are members of the organization, and other celebrities could be attracted to the cause. Many Grand Army members are wary of this approach, however: in the past, the net receipts of some fund-raising efforts have been relatively insignificant, given the costs of staging them.

A third approach, suggested by many of the younger members, is to have new applicants share some of the costs of construction and maintenance. The spouses and children would pay an up-front "enrollment" fee, based on a sliding scale proportionate to their income and assets, and then a monthly fee adjusted similarly to contribute to maintenance costs. Many older members are strongly opposed to this idea, as it is in direct contradiction to the principles on which the organization was founded more than a century ago.

The fourth option is simply to maintain the status quo, focus the organization's efforts on supporting the families who already live at the National Home, and wait to accept new applicants based on attrition.

CONCLUSION: At its annual national convention, the Grand Army of Foreign Wars votes to impose a one-time tax of $10 on each member for the purpose of expanding and supporting the National Home to welcome a larger number of applicants. The tax is considered to be the solution most likely to produce the funds needed to accommodate the growing number of applicants.

10. Actuarial studies have shown that because the Grand Army's membership consists mostly of older veterans from earlier wars, the organization's membership will suffer a precipitous decline in numbers in about five years. 10.__

   A.
   B.
   C.
   D.
   E.

11. After passage of the funding measure, a splinter group of older members appeals for the "sliding scale" provision to be applied to the tax, so that some members may be allowed to contribute less based on their income. 11.__

   A.
   B.
   C.
   D.
   E.

12. The original charter of the Grand Army of Foreign Wars specifically states that the organization will not levy any taxes or duties on its members beyond its modest annual dues. It takes a super-majority of attending delegates at the national convention to make alterations to the charter.

     12.____

     A.
     B.
     C.
     D.
     E.

13. Six months before Grand Army of Foreign Wars' national convention, the Internal Revenue Service rules that because it is an organization that engages in political lobbying, the Grand Army must no longer enjoy its own federal tax-exempt status.

     13.____

     A.
     B.
     C.
     D.
     E.

14. Two months before the national convention, Dirk Rockwell, arguably the country's most famous film actor, announces in a nationally televised interview that he has been saddened to learn of the plight of the National Home, and that he is going to make it his own personal crusade to see that it is able to house and support a greater number of widowed spouses and orphans in the future.

     14.____

     A.
     B.
     C.
     D.
     E.

15. The Grand Army's final estimate is that the cost of expanding the National Home to accommodate the increased number of applicants will be about $61 million.

     15.____

     A.
     B.
     C.
     D.
     E.

16. Just before the national convention, the federal Department of Veterans Affairs announces steep cuts in the benefits package that is currently offered to the widowed spouses and orphans of veterans.

     16.____

     A.
     B.
     C.
     D.

17. After the national convention, the Grand Army of Foreign Wars begins charging a modest   17.___
    "start-up" fee to all families who apply for residence at the national home.

    A.
    B.
    C.
    D.
    E.

Questions 18-25.

DIRECTIONS: Questions 18-25 each provide four factual statements and a conclusion based
              on these statements. After reading the entire question, you will decide
              whether:
              A.   The conclusion is proved by statements 1-4;
              B.   The conclusion is disproved by statements 1-4; or
              C.   The facts are not sufficient to prove or disprove the conclusion.

18.   FACTUAL STATEMENTS: 18.___

      1. In the Field Day high jump competition, Martha jumped higher than Frank.
      2. Carl jumped higher than Ignacio.
      3. Ignacio jumped higher than Frank.
      4. Dan jumped higher than Carl.

      CONCLUSION: Frank finished last in the high jump competition.

      A.   The conclusion is proved by statements 1-4.
      B.   The conclusion is disproved by statements 1-4.
      C.   The facts are not sufficient to prove or disprove the conclusion.

19.   FACTUAL STATEMENTS: 19.___

      1. The door to the hammer mill chamber is locked if light 6 is red.
      2. The door to the hammer mill chamber is locked only when the mill is operating.
      3. If the mill is not operating, light 6 is blue.
      4. Light 6 is blue.

      CONCLUSION: The door to the hammer mill chamber is locked.

      A.   The conclusion is proved by statements 1-4.
      B.   The conclusion is disproved by statements 1-4.
      C.   The facts are not sufficient to prove or disprove the conclusion.

20. FACTUAL STATEMENTS: 20._____

   1. Ziegfried, the lion tamer at the circus, has demanded ten additional minutes of performance time during each show.
   2. If Ziegfried is allowed his ten additional minutes per show, he will attempt to teach Kimba the tiger to shoot a basketball.
   3. If Kimba learns how to shoot a basketball, then Ziegfried was not given his ten additional minutes.
   4. Ziegfried was given his ten additional minutes.

CONCLUSION: Despite Ziegfried's efforts, Kimba did not learn how to shoot a basketball.

   A. The conclusion is proved by statements 1-4.
   B. The conclusion is disproved by statements 1-4.
   C. The facts are not sufficient to prove or disprove the conclusion.

21. FACTUAL STATEMENTS: 21._____

   1. If Stan goes to counseling, Sara won't divorce him.
   2. If Sara divorces Stan, she'll move back to Texas.
   3. If Sara doesn't divorce Stan, Irene will be disappointed.
   4. Stan goes to counseling.

CONCLUSION: Irene will be disappointed.

   A. The conclusion is proved by statements 1-4.
   B. The conclusion is disproved by statements 1-4.
   C. The facts are not sufficient to prove or disprove the conclusion.

22. FACTUAL STATEMENTS: 22._____

   1. If Delia is promoted to district manager, Claudia will have to be promoted to team leader.
   2. Delia will be promoted to district manager unless she misses her fourth-quarter sales quota.
   3. If Claudia is promoted to team leader, Thomas will be promoted to assistant team leader.
   4. Delia meets her fourth-quarter sales quota.

CONCLUSION: Thomas is promoted to assistant team leader.

   A. The conclusion is proved by statements 1-4.
   B. The conclusion is disproved by statements 1-4.
   C. The facts are not sufficient to prove or disprove the conclusion.

23. FACTUAL STATEMENTS: 23.___

    1. Clone D is identical to Clone B.
    2. Clone B is not identical to Clone A.
    3. Clone D is not identical to Clone C.
    4. Clone E is not identical to the clones that are identical to Clone B.

CONCLUSION: Clone E is identical to Clone D.

    A. The conclusion is proved by statements 1-4.
    B. The conclusion is disproved by statements 1-4.
    C. The facts are not sufficient to prove or disprove the conclusion.

24. FACTUAL STATEMENTS: 24.___

    1. In the Stafford Tower, each floor is occupied by a single business.
    2. Big G Staffing is on a floor between CyberGraphics and MainEvent.
    3. Gasco is on the floor directly below CyberGraphics and three floors above Treehorn Audio.
    4. MainEvent is five floors below EZ Tax and four floors below Treehorn Audio.

CONCLUSION: EZ Tax is on a floor between Gasco and MainEvent.

    A. The conclusion is proved by statements 1-4.
    B. The conclusion is disproved by statements 1-4.
    C. The facts are not sufficient to prove or disprove the conclusion.

25. FACTUAL STATEMENTS: 25.___

    1. Only county roads lead to Nicodemus.
    2. All the roads from Hill City to Graham County are federal highways.
    3. Some of the roads from Plainville lead to Nicodemus.
    4. Some of the roads running from Hill City lead to Strong City.

CONCLUSION: Some of the roads from Plainville are county roads.

    A. The conclusion is proved by statements 1-4.
    B. The conclusion is disproved by statements 1-4.
    C. The facts are not sufficient to prove or disprove the conclusion.

KEY (CORRECT ANSWERS)

1.	A		11.	A
2.	A		12.	D
3.	A		13.	E
4.	C		14.	D
5.	A		15.	B
6.	B		16.	B
7.	A		17.	C
8.	A		18.	A
9.	A		19.	B
10.	E		20.	A

21.	A
22.	A
23.	B
24.	A
25.	A

___

SOLUTIONS TO PROBLEMS

1) (A) Given statement 3, we deduce that James will not be transferred to another department. By statement 2, we can conclude that James will be promoted.

2) (A) Since every player on the softball team wears glasses, these individuals compose some of the people who work at the bank. Although not every person who works at the bank plays softball, those bank employees who do play softball wear glasses.

3) (A) If Henry and June go out to dinner, we conclude that it must be on Tuesday or Thursday, which are the only two days when they have childbirth classes. This implies that if it is not Tuesday or Thursday, then this couple does not go out to dinner.

4) (C) We can only conclude that if a person plays on the field hockey team, then he or she has both bruises and scarred knees. But there are probably a great number of people who have both bruises and scarred knees but do not play on the field hockey team. The given conclusion can neither be proven or disproven.

5) (A) From statement 1, if Jane beats Mathias, then Lance will beat Jane. Using statement 2, we can then conclude that Christine will not win her match against Jane.

6) (B) Statement 1 tells us that no green light can be an indicator of the belt drive status. Thus, the given conclusion must be false.

7) (A) We already know that Ben and Elliot are in the 7th grade. Even though Hannah and Carl are in the same grade, it cannot be the 7th grade because we would then have at least four students in this 7th grade. This would contradict the third statement, which states that either two or three students are in each grade. Since Amy, Dan, and Francine are in different grades, exactly one of them must be in the 7th grade. Thus, Ben, Elliot and exactly one of Amy, Dan, and Francine are the three students in the 7th grade.

8) (A) One man is a teacher, who is Russian. We know that the writer is female and is Russian. Since her husband is an engineer, he cannot be the Russian teacher. Thus, her husband is of German descent, namely Mr. Stern. This means that Mr. Stern's wife is the writer. Note that one couple consists of a male Russian teacher and a female German lawyer. The other couple consists of a male German engineer and a female Russian writer.

9) (A) Since John is more than 10 inches taller than Lisa, his height is at least 46 inches. Also, John is shorter than Henry, so Henry's height must be greater than 46 inches. Thus, Lisa is the only one whose height is less than 36 inches. Therefore, she is the only one who is not allowed on the flume ride.

18) (A) Dan jumped higher than Carl, who jumped higher than Ignacio, who jumped higher than Frank. Since Martha jumped higher than Frank, every person jumped higher than Frank. Thus, Frank finished last.

19) (B) If the light is red, then the door is locked. If the door is locked, then the mill is operating. Reversing the logical sequence of these statements, if the mill is not operating, then the door is not locked, which means that the light is blue. Thus, the given conclusion is disproved.

20) (A) Using the contrapositive of statement 3, if Ziegfried was given his ten additional minutes, then Kimba did not learn how to shoot a basketball. Since statement 4 is factual, the conclusion is proved.

21) (A) From statements 4 and 1, we conclude that Sara doesn't divorce Stan. Then statement 3 reveals that Irene will be disappointed. Thus the conclusion is proved.

22) (A) Statement 2 can be rewritten as "Delia is promoted to district manager or she misses her sales quota." Furthermore, this statement is equivalent to "If Delia makes her sales quota, then she is promoted to district manager." From statement 1, we conclude that Claudia is promoted to team leader. Finally, by statement 3, Thomas is promoted to assistant team leader. The conclusion is proved.

23) (B) By statement 4, Clone E is not identical to any clones identical to clone B. Statement 1 tells us that clones B and D are identical. Therefore, clone E cannot be identical to clone D. The conclusion is disproved.

24) (A) Based on all four statements, CyberGraphics is somewhere below Main Event. Gasco is one floor below CyberGraphics. EZ Tax is two floors below Gasco. Treehorn Audio is one floor below EZ Tax. Main Event is four floors below Treehorn Audio. Thus, EZ Tax is two floors below Gasco and five floors above Main Event. The conclusion is proved.

25) (A) From statement 3, we know that some of the roads from Plainville lead to Nicodemus. But statement 1 tells us that only county roads lead to Nicodemus. Therefore, some of the roads from Plainville must be county roads. The conclusion is proved.

TEST 2

DIRECTIONS: Each question or incomplete statement is followed by several suggested answers or completions. Select the one that BEST answers the question or completes the statement. *PRINT THE LETTER OF THE CORRECT ANSWER IN THE SPACE AT THE RIGHT.*

Questions 1-9.

DIRECTIONS: In questions 1-9, you will read a set of facts and a conclusion drawn from them. The conclusion may be valid or invalid, based on the facts-it's your task to determine the validity of the conclusion.

For each question, select the letter before the statement that BEST expresses the relationship between the given facts and the conclusion that has been drawn from them. Your choices are:
A. The facts prove the conclusion
B. The facts disprove the conclusion; or
C. The facts neither prove nor disprove the conclusion.

1. FACTS: Some employees in the testing department are statisticians. Most of the statisti-   1.___
cians who work in the testing department are projection specialists. Tom Wilks works in
the testing department.

   CONCLUSION: Tom Wilks is a statistician.

   A. The facts prove the conclusion.
   B. The facts disprove the conclusion.
   C. The facts neither prove nor disprove the conclusion.

2. FACTS: Ten coins are split among Hank, Lawrence, and Gail. If Lawrence gives his coins   2.___
to Hank, then Hank will have more coins than Gail. If Gail gives her coins to Lawrence,
then Lawrence will have more coins than Hank.

   CONCLUSION: Hank has six coins.

   A. The facts prove the conclusion.
   B. The facts disprove the conclusion.
   C. The facts neither prove nor disprove the conclusion.

3. FACTS: Nobody loves everybody. Janet loves Ken. Ken loves everybody who loves   3.___
Janet.

   CONCLUSION: Everybody loves Janet.

   A. The facts prove the conclusion.
   B. The facts disprove the conclusion.
   C. The facts neither prove nor disprove the conclusion.

4. FACTS: Most of the Torres family lives in East Los Angeles. Many people in East Los Angeles celebrate Cinco de Mayo. Joe is a member of the Torres family.

    CONCLUSION: Joe lives in East Los Angeles.

    A. The facts prove the conclusion.
    B. The facts disprove the conclusion.
    C. The facts neither prove nor disprove the conclusion.

4.____

5. FACTS: Five professionals each occupy one story of a five-story office building. Dr. Kane's office is above Dr. Assad's. Dr. Johnson's office is between Dr. Kane's and Dr. Conlon's. Dr. Steen's office is between Dr. Conlon's and Dr. Assad's. Dr. Johnson is on the fourth story.

    CONCLUSION: Dr. Kane occupies the top story.

    A. The facts prove the conclusion.
    B. The facts disprove the conclusion.
    C. The facts neither prove nor disprove the conclusion.

5.____

6. FACTS: To be eligible for membership in the Yukon Society, a person must be able to either tunnel through a snowbank while wearing only a T-shirt and shorts, or hold his breath for two minutes under water that is 50° F. Ray can only hold his breath for a minute and a half.

    CONCLUSION: Ray can still become a member of the Yukon Society by tunneling through a snowbank while wearing a T-shirt and shorts.

    A. The facts prove the conclusion.
    B. The facts disprove the conclusion.
    C. The facts neither prove nor disprove the conclusion.

6.____

7. FACTS: A mark is worth five plunks. You can exchange four sharps for a tinplot. It takes eight marks to buy a sharp.

    CONCLUSION: A sharp is the most valuable.

    A. The facts prove the conclusion.
    B. The facts disprove the conclusion.
    C. The facts neither prove nor disprove the conclusion.

7.____

8. FACTS: There are gibbons, as well as lemurs, who like to play in the trees at the monkey house. All those who like to play in the trees at the monkey house are fed lettuce and bananas.

    CONCLUSION: Lemurs and gibbons are types of monkeys.

    A. The facts prove the conclusion.
    B. The facts disprove the conclusion.
    C. The facts neither prove nor disprove the conclusion.

8.____

9. FACTS: None of the Blackfoot tribes is a Salishan Indian tribe. Sal-ishan Indians came from the northern Pacific Coast. All Salishan Indians live east of the Continental Divide.

9.___

CONCLUSION: No Blackfoot tribes live east of the Continental Divide.

   A. The facts prove the conclusion.
   B. The facts disprove the conclusion.
   C. The facts neither prove nor disprove the conclusion.

Questions 10-17.

DIRECTIONS: Questions 10-17 are based on the following reading passage. It is not your knowledge of the particular topic that is being tested, but your ability to reason based on what you have read. The passage is likely to detail several proposed courses of action and factors affecting these proposals. The reading passage is followed by a conclusion or outcome based on the facts in the passage, or a description of a decision taken regarding the situation. The conclusion is followed by a number of statements that have a possible connection to the conclusion. For each statement, you are to determine whether:

   A. The statement proves the conclusion.
   B. The statement supports the conclusion but does not prove it.
   C. The statement disproves the conclusion.
   D. The statement weakens the conclusion but does not disprove it.
   E. The statement has no relevance to the conclusion.

Remember that the conclusion after the passage is to be accepted as the outcome of what actually happened, and that you are being asked to evaluate the impact each statement would have had on the conclusion.

PASSAGE:

On August 12, Beverly Willey reported that she was in the elevator late on the previous evening after leaving her office on the 16th floor of a large office building. In her report, she states that a man got on the elevator at the 11th floor, pulled her off the elevator, assaulted her, and stole her purse. Ms. Willey reported that she had seen the man in the elevators and hallways of the building before. She believes that the man works in the building. Her description of him is as follows: he is tall, unshaven, with wavy brown hair and a scar on his left cheek. He walks with a pronounced limp, often dragging his left foot behind his right.

CONCLUSION: After Beverly Willey makes her report, the police arrest a 43-year-man, Barton Black, and charge him with her assault.

10. Barton Black is a former Marine who served in Vietnam, where he sustained shrapnel wounds to the left side of his face and suffered nerve damage in his left leg.

10.___

   A.
   B.
   C.
   D.
   E.

11. When they arrived at his residence to question him, detectives were greeted at the door   11.____
    by Barton Black, who was tall and clean-shaven.

    A.
    B.
    C.
    D.
    E.

12. Barton Black was booked into the county jail several days after Beverly Willey's assault.   12.____

    A.
    B.
    C.
    D.
    E.

13. Upon further investigation, detectives discover that Beverly Willey does not work at the   13.____
    office building.

    A.
    B.
    C.
    D.
    E.

14. Upon further investigation, detectives discover that Barton Black does not work at the   14.____
    office building.

    A.
    B.
    C.
    D.
    E.

15. In the spring of the following year, Barton Black is convicted of assaulting Beverly Willey   15.____
    on August 11.

    A.
    B.
    C.
    D.
    E.

16. During their investigation of the assault, detectives determine that Beverly Willey was   16.____
    assaulted on the 12th floor of the office building.

    A.
    B.
    C.
    D.
    E.

17. The day after Beverly Willey's assault, Barton Black fled the area and was never seen   17.__
     again.

     A.
     B.
     C.
     D.
     E.

Questions 18-25.

DIRECTIONS: Questions 18-25 each provide four factual statements and a conclusion based
               on these statements. After reading the entire question, you will decide
               whether:

               A. The conclusion is proved by statements 1-4;
               B. The conclusion is disproved by statements 1-4; or
               C. The facts are not sufficient to prove or disprove the conclusion.

18. FACTUAL STATEMENTS: 18.__

     1. Among five spice jars on the shelf, the sage is to the right of the parsley.
     2. The pepper is to the left of the basil.
     3. The nutmeg is between the sage and the pepper.
     4. The pepper is the second spice from the left.

     CONCLUSION: The sage is the farthest to the right.

     A. The conclusion is proved by statements 1-4.
     B. The conclusion is disproved by statements 1-4.
     C. The facts are not sufficient to prove or disprove the conclusion.

19. FACTUAL STATEMENTS: 19.__

     1. Gear X rotates in a clockwise direction if Switch C is in the OFF position
     2. Gear X will rotate in a counter-clockwise direction if Switch C is ON.
     3. If Gear X is rotating in a clockwise direction, then Gear Y will not be rotating at all.
     4. Switch C is ON.

     CONCLUSION: Gear X is rotating in a counter-clockwise direction.

     A. The conclusion is proved by statements 1-4.
     B. The conclusion is disproved by statements 1-4.
     C. The facts are not sufficient to prove or disprove the conclusion.

20. FACTUAL STATEMENTS: 20.____
    1. Lane will leave for the Toronto meeting today only if Terence, Rourke, and Jackson all
       file their marketing reports by the end of the work day.
    2. Rourke will file her report on time only if Ganz submits last quarter's data.
    3. If Terence attends the security meeting, he will attend it with Jackson, and they will not
       file their marketing reports by the end of the work day.
    4. Ganz submits last quarter's data to Rourke.

    CONCLUSION: Lane will leave for the Toronto meeting today.

    A. The conclusion is proved by statements 1-4.
    B. The conclusion is disproved by statements 1-4.
    C. The facts are not sufficient to prove or disprove the conclusion.

21. FACTUAL STATEMENTS: 21.____

    1. Bob is in second place in the Boston Marathon.
    2. Gregory is winning the Boston Marathon.
    3. There are four miles to go in the race, and Bob is gaining on Gregory at the rate of
       100 yards every minute.
    4. There are 1760 yards in a mile, and Gregory's usual pace during the Boston Mara-
       thon is one mile every six minutes.

    CONCLUSION: Bob wins the Boston Marathon.

    A. The conclusion is proved by statements 1-4.
    B. The conclusion is disproved by statements 1-4.
    C. The facts are not sufficient to prove or disprove the conclusion.

22. FACTUAL STATEMENTS: 22.____

    1. Four brothers are named Earl, John, Gary, and Pete.
    2. Earl and Pete are unmarried.
    3. John is shorter than the youngest of the four.
    4. The oldest brother is married, and is also the tallest.

    CONCLUSION: Gary is the oldest brother.

    A. The conclusion is proved by statements 1-4.
    B. The conclusion is disproved by statements 1-4.
    C. The facts are not sufficient to prove or disprove the conclusion.

23. FACTUAL STATEMENTS: 23.____

    1. Brigade X is ten miles from the demilitarized zone.
    2. If General Woundwort gives the order, Brigade X will advance to the demilitarized
       zone, but not quickly enough to reach the zone before the conflict begins.
    3. Brigade Y, five miles behind Brigade X, will not advance unless General Woundwort
       gives the order.
    4. Brigade Y advances.

    CONCLUSION: Brigade X reaches the demilitarized zone before the conflict begins.

A. The conclusion is proved by statements 1-4.
B. The conclusion is disproved by statements 1-4.
C. The facts are not sufficient to prove or disprove the conclusion.

24. FACTUAL STATEMENTS: 24.__

1. Jerry has decided to take a cab from Fullerton to Elverton.
2. Chubby Cab charges $5 plus $3 a mile.
3. Orange Cab charges $7.50 but gives free mileage for the first 5 miles.
4. After the first 5 miles, Orange Cab charges $2.50 a mile.

CONCLUSION: Orange Cab is the cheaper fare from Fullerton to Elverton.

A. The conclusion is proved by statements 1-4.
B. The conclusion is disproved by statements 1-4.
C. The facts are not sufficient to prove or disprove the conclusion.

25. FACTUAL STATEMENTS: 25.__

1. Dan is never in class when his friend Lucy is absent.
2. Lucy is never absent unless her mother is sick.
3. If Lucy is in class, Sergio is in class also
4. Sergio is never in class when Dalton is absent.

CONCLUSION: If Lucy is absent, Dalton may be in class.

A. The conclusion is proved by statements 1-4.
B. The conclusion is disproved by statements 1-4.
C. The facts are not sufficient to prove or disprove the conclusion.

KEY (CORRECT ANSWERS)

1.	C		11.	E
2.	B		12.	B
3.	B		13.	D
4.	C		14.	E
5.	A		15.	A
6.	A		16.	E
7.	B		17.	C
8.	C		18.	B
9.	C		19.	A
10.	B		20.	C

21. C
22. A
23. B
24. A
25. B

———

SOLUTIONS TO PROBLEMS

1) (C) Statement 1 only tells us that some employees who work in the Testing Department are statisticians. This means that we need to allow the possibility that at least one person in this department is not a statistician. Thus, if a person works in the Testing Department, we cannot conclude whether or not this individual is a statistician.

2) (B) If Hank had six coins, then the total of Gails collection and Lawrence's collection would be four. Thus, if Gail gave all her coins to Lawrence, Lawrence would only have four coins. Thus, it would be impossible for Lawrence to have more coins than Hank.

3) (B) Statement 1 tells us that nobody loves everybody. If everybody loved Janet, then Statement 3 would imply that Ken loves everybody. This would contradict statement 1. The conclusion is disproved.

4) (C) Although most of the Torres family lives in East Los Angeles, we can assume that some members of this family do not live in East Los Angeles. Thus, we cannot prove or disprove that Joe, who is a member of the Torres family, lives in East Los Angeles.

5) (A) Since Dr. Johnson is on the 4th floor, either (a) Dr. Kane is on the 5th floor and Dr. Conlon is on the 3rd floor, or (b) Dr. Kane is on the 3rd floor and Dr. Conlon is on the 5th floor. If option (b) were correct, then since Dr. Assad would be on the 1st floor, it would be impossible for Dr. Steen's office to be between Dr. Conlon and Dr. Assad's office. Therefore, Dr. Kane's office must be on the 5th floor. The order of the doctors' offices, from 5th floor down to the 1st floor is: Dr. Kane, Dr. Johnson, Dr. Conlon, Dr. Steen, Dr. Assad.

6) (A) Ray does not satisfy the requirement of holding his breath for two minutes under water, since he can only hold his breath for one minute in that setting. But if he tunnels through a snowbank with just a T-shirt and shorts, he will satisfy the eligibility requirement. Note that the eligibility requirement contains the key word "or." So only one of the two clauses separated by "or" need to be fulfilled.

7) (B) Statement 2 says that four sharps is equivalent to one tinplot. This means that a tinplot is worth more than a sharp. The conclusion is disproved. We note that the order of these items, from most valuable to least valuable are: tinplot, sharp, mark, plunk.

8) (C) We can only conclude that gibbons and lemurs are fed lettuce and bananas. We can neither prove or disprove that these animals are types of monkeys.

9) (C) We know that all Salishan Indians live east of the Continental Divide. But some nonmembers of this tribe of Indians may also live east of the Continental Divide. Since none of the members of the Blackfoot tribe belong to the Salishan Indian tribe, we cannot draw any conclusion about the location of the Blackfoot tribe with respect to the Continental Divide.

18) (B) Since the pepper is second from the left and the nutmeg is between the sage and the pepper, the positions 2, 3, and 4 (from the left) are pepper, nutmeg, sage. By statement 2, the basil must be in position 5, which implies that the parsley is in position 1. Therefore, the basil, not the sage is farthest to the right. The conclusion disproved.

19) (A) Statement 2 assures us that if switch C is ON, then Gear X is rotating in a counterclockwise direction. The conclusion is proved.

20) (C) Based on Statement 4, followed by Statement 2, we conclude that Ganz and Rourke will file their reports on time. Statement 3 reveals that if Terence and Jackson attend the security meeting, they will fail to file their reports on time. We have no further information if Terence and Jackson attended the security meeting, so we are not able to either confirm or deny that their reports were filed on time. This implies that we cannot know for certain that Lane will leave for his meeting in Toronto.

21) (C) Although Bob is in second place behind Gregory, we cannot deduce how far behind Gregory he is running. At Gregory's current pace, he will cover four miles in 24 minutes. If Bob were only 100 yards behind Gregory, he would catch up to Gregory in one minute. But if Bob were very far behind Gregory, for example 5 miles, this is the equivalent of (5)(1760) = 8800 yards. Then Bob would need 8800/100 = 88 minutes to catch up to Gregory. Thus, the given facts are not sufficient to draw a conclusion.

22) (A) Statement 2 tells us that neither Earl nor Pete could be the oldest; also, either John or Gary is married. Statement 4 reveals that the oldest brother is both married and the tallest. By statement 3, John cannot be the tallest. Since John is not the tallest, he is not the oldest. Thus, the oldest brother must be Gary. The conclusion is proved.

23) (B) By statements 3 and 4, General Woundwort must have given the order to advance. Statement 2 then tells us that Brigade X will advance to the demilitarized zone, but not soon enough before the conflict begins. Thus, the conclusion is disproved.

24) (A) If the distance is 5 miles or less, then the cost for the Orange Cab is only $7.50, whereas the cost for the Chubby Cab is $5 + 3x, where x represents the number of miles traveled. For 1 to 5 miles, the cost of the Chubby Cab is between $8 and $20. This means that for a distance of 5 miles, the Orange Cab costs $7.50, whereas the Chubby Cab costs $20. After 5 miles, the cost per mile of the Chubby Cab exceeds the cost per mile of the Orange Cab. Thus, regardless of the actual distance between Fullerton and Elverton, the cost for the Orange Cab will be cheaper than that of the Chubby Cab.

25) (B) It looks like "Dalton" should be replaced by "Dan in the conclusion. Then by statement 1, if Lucy is absent, Dan is never in class. Thus, the conclusion is disproved.

BASIC FUNDAMENTALS OF LIBRARY SCIENCE

TABLE OF CONTENTS

BASIC FUNDAMENTALS OF LIBRARY SCIENCE

The problem of classifying' all human knowledge has produced a branch of learning called "library science." A lasting contribution to a simple and understandable method of locating a book on any topic was designed by Melvil Dewey in 1876. His plan divided all knowledge into ten large classes and then dubdivided each class according to related groups.

DEWEY DECIMAL SYSTEM

1. Subject Classification

   The Dewey Decimal Classification System is the accepted and most widely used subject classification system in libraries throughout the world.

2. Classification by Three (3) Groups

   There are three groups of classification in the system. A basic group of ten (10) classifications arranges all knowledge as represented by books within groups by classifications numbered 000-900.

   The second group is the "100 division"; each group of the basic "10 divisions" is again divided into 9 sub-sctions allowing for more detailed and specialized subjects not identified in the 10 basic divisions.

3. There is a third, still further specialized "One thousand" group where each of the "100" classifications are further divided by decimalized, more specified, subject classifications. The "1,000" group is mainly used by highly specialized scientific and much diversified libraries.

   These are the subject classes of the Dewey System:

000-099   General works (included bibliography, encyclopedias, collections, periodicals, newspapers,etc.)

100-199   Philosophy (includes psychology, logic, ethics, conduct, etc.) 200-299 Religion (includes mythology, natural theology, Bible, church history, etc.)

300-399   Social Science (includes economics, government, law, education, commerce, etc.)

400-499   Language (includes dictionaries, grammars, philology, etc.) 500-599 Science (includes mathematics, chemistry, physics, astronomy, geology, etc.) 600-699 Useful Arts (includes agriculture, engineering, aviation, medicine, manufactures, etc.) 700-799 Fine Arts (includes sculpture, painting, music, photography, gardening, etc.)

800-899   Literature (includes poetry, plays, orations, etc.) 900-999 History (includes geoegraphy, travel, biography, ancient and modern history, etc.)

PREPARING TO USE THE LIBRARY

Your ability to use the library and its resources is an important factor in determining your success. Skill and efficiency in finding the library materials you need for assignments and research papers will increase the amount of time you have to devote to reading or organizing information.

These are some of the preparations you can make now.

1. Develop skill in using your local library. You can increase your familiarity with the card catalog and the periodical indexes,such as the *Readers' Guide to Periodical Literature, in* any library.
2. Take the *Test in Library Science* to see how you can improve your knowledge of the library.
3. Read in such books as *Books, Libraries and You* by Jessie Edna Boyd, *The Library Key* by Margaret G.Cook, and *Making Books Work, a Guide to the Use of Libraries* by Jennie Maas Flexner.

You can find other titles by looking under the subject heading LIBRARIES AND READERS in the card catalog of your library. THREE TYPES OF BOOK CARDS

Here are the three general types of cards which are used to represent a book in the main catalog.

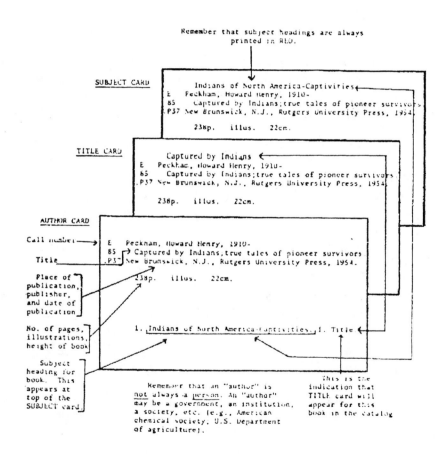

CARD CATALOG

The Card Catalog lists all books in the library by author. The majority of books also have title and subject cards.

Author card

If the author is known, look in the catalog under the author's name. The "author" for some works may be a society, an institution, or a government department.

Title card

Books with distinctive titles, anonymous works and periodicals will have a title card.

Subject card

To find books on a specific subject, look in the catalog under that subject heading. (Subject headings are printed in red on the Catalog Card.)

Call number

The letters and numbers in the upper left-hand corner *of the* Catalog Card are the book's call number. Copy this call number accurately, for it will determine the shelf location of the book. The word "Reference" marked in red in the upper right-hand corner of the catalog card indicates that the item is shelved in the Reference Section,and "Periodical "marked in yellow on the Catalog Card indicates that the item is shelved in the Periodicals Section. PERIODICALS

All magazines are arranged in alphabetical order by title. PERIODICALS FILE

To determine whether the Library has a specific magazine, consult the Periodicals File. Check the title of the magazine needed, and note that there are two cards for each title.

The bottom card lists the current issues available. The top card lists back bound volumes.

Those marked "Ask at Ref.Desk" may be obtained from the Reference Librarian. PERIODICAL INDEXES

Material in magazines is more up-to-date than books and is a valuable source of information. To find articles on a chosen subject, use the periodical indexes.

The Readers' Guide to Periodical Literature is the most familiar of these indexes. In the front of each volume is a list of the periodicals indexed and a key to abbreviations. Similar aids appear in the front of other periodical indexes.

Sample entry: WEASELS

              WONDERFUL WHITE WEASEL. R.Beck. il OUTDOOR LIFE 135:48-9+
          Ja '65

Explanation :   An illustrated article on the subject WEASELS entitled WONDERFUL WHITE
               WEASEL, by R.Beck,will be found in volume 135 of OUTDOOR LIFE, pages
               48-9 (continued on later pages of the same issue), the January 1965 number.
Major libraries subscribe to the following indexes:

Art Index
Biography Index
Book Review Index
British Humanities Index
Essay and General Literature Index
    This is helpful for locating criticism of works of literature.
An Index to Book Reviews in the Humanities
International Index ceased publications June, 1965 and continued as Social Science and
    Humanities Index
The Music Index The New York
Times Index Nineteenth Century Readers' Guide
Poole's Index
Poverty and Human Resources Abstracts
Psychological Abstracts
Public Affairs Information Service.Bulletin of the (PAIS) is a subject index to current
    books,pamphlets,periodical articles, government documents, and other library materials
    in economics and public affairs.

4

Readers' Guide to Periodical Literature
Social Science and Humanities Index a continuation of the International Index
Sociological Abstracts

Do you have the basic skills for using a library efficiently? You should be able to answer AT LEAST 33 of the following questions correctly. *CHECK YOUR ANSWERS BY TURNING TO THE ANSWER KEY AT THE BACK OF THIS SECTION.*
USING A CARD CATALOG
Questions 1-9.

DIRECTIONS: An author card (or "main entry" card) is shown below. Identify each item on the card by selecting the CORRECT letters for them. *PRINT THE LETTER OF THE CORRECT ANSWER IN THE SPACE AT THE RIGHT.*

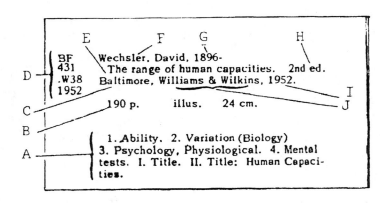

Sample Answer:

0.   F

1.   Date book was published.   1.

2.   Number of pages in book.   2.

3.   Title.   3.

4.   Place of publication.   4.

5.   Call number.   5.

6.   Year author was born   6.

7.   Edition.   7.

8.   Publisher.   8.

9.   Other headings under which cards for this book may be found.   9.

Questions 10-13.

DIRECTIONS: Select the letter preceding the word or phrase which completes each of the following statements correctly.

10. The library's title card for the book THE LATE GEORGE APLEY can be found by looking in the card catalog under   10.____

    A. Apley, George   B. The   C. Late   D. George   E. Apley

11. A catalog card for a book by John F. Kennedy would be found in the drawer labelled   11.____

    A. JEFFERSON-JOHNSON,ROY
    B. PRESCOTT-PRICELESS
    C. KIERNAN-KLAY
    D. U.S.PRESIDENT-U.S.SOCIAL SECURITY
    E. KENNEBEC-KIERKEGAARD

12. The title cards for these three periodicals would be found in the card catalog arranged in which of the following orders: 12.____

    A. NEW YORKER, NEWSWEEK, NEW YORK TIMES MAGAZINE
    B. NEWSWEEK, NEW YORKER, NEW YORK TIMES MAGAZINE
    C. NEW YORK TIMES MAGAZINE, NEW YORKER, NEWSWEEK
    D. NEW YORKER, NEW YORK TIMES MAGAZINE, NEWSWEEK
    E. NEWSWEEK, NEW YORK TIMES MAGAZINE, NEW YORKER

13. A card for a copy of the U.N.Charter would be found in the catalog drawer marked   13.____

    A. TWENTIETH-UNAMUNO
    B. UNITED MINE WORKERS-UNITED SHOE MACHINERY
    C. U.S.BUREAU-U.S. CONGRESS
    D. U.S.SOCIAL POLICY-UNIVERSITAS
    E. CHANCEL-CIARDI

II. UNDERSTANDING ENTRIES IN A PERIODICAL INDEX

Questions 14-25.

DIRECTIONS: The following items are excerpts from THE READERS' GUIDE TO PERIODICAL LITERATURE. Identify each lettered section of the entries by placing the correct letters in the spaces.(There are more letters than spaces, so some of the letters will not be used.)

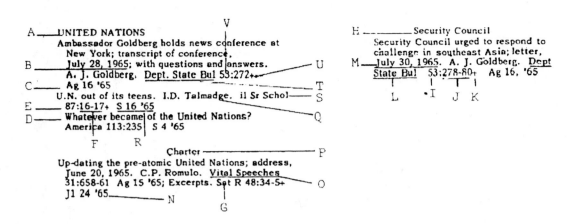

14. Title of magazine containing a transcript of a news con-conference held by U.N. Ambassador Arthur Goldberg.   14.__

15. Magazine in which the full text of C.P. Romulo's address on the U.N. appears.   15.__

16. Author of an article titled U.N. OUT OF ITS TEENS.   16.__

17. Date on which Ambassador Goldberg wrote a letter urging the Security Council to respond to the challenge of southeast Asia.   17.__

18. Title of an article for which no author is listed.   18.__

19. Date of the SATURDAY REVIEW issue which contains excerptsl of a speech called "Up-Dating the Pre-Atomic United Nations."   19.__

20. Pages in the DEPARTMENT OF STATE BULLETIN on which Ambassador Goldberg's letter appears.   20.__

21. Symbol indicating that the letter is continued on a later page.   21.__

22. Volume number of the magazine in which the article by I.D. Talmadge is printed.   22.__

23. Symbols meaning September 16, 1965.   23.__

24. The general subject heading under which all five articles are listed.   24.__

25. A subject heading subdivision.   25.__

Questions 26-27.

DIRECTIONS: Select the letter preceding the phrase which completes each of the following statements correctly.

26. To determine whether or not the library has THE MAGAZINE OF AMERICAN HISTORY, check in   26.__

    A.   the list of magazine titles in the front of THE READERS' GUIDE TO PERIODICAL LITERATURE
    B.   the library's card catalog

C. Ulrich's GUIDE TO PERIODICALS
D. SATURDAY REVIEW
E. THE LIBRARY JOURNAL

27. THE READERS' GUIDE is a good place to look for material on the Job Corps because it   27.____

    A. indexes only the best books and magazines in each field
    B. is a guide to articles on many subjects appearing in all of the library's periodicals
    C. indexes recent discussions on the subject in many magazines
    D. specializes in official government information
    E. does all of the above

III. IDENTIFYING LIBRARY TERMS

Questions 28-32.

DIRECTIONS: Match the correct definitions with these terms by placing the correct letters in the blanks. (Some of the letters will not be used.)

28. Bibliography   A. Word or phrase printed in A. Word or phrase printed in log to indicate the major log to indicate the major   28.____

29. Anthology   B. Brief written summary of the major ideas presented in an article or book   29.____

30. Index   C. List of books and/or articles on one subject or by one author   30.____

31. Abstract   D. Collection of selections from the writings of one or several authors   31.____

32. Subject heading   E. Written account of a person's life   32.____

F. Alphabetical list of subjects with the pages on which they are to be found in a book or periodical

G. Subordinate, usually explanatory title, additional to the main title and usually printed below it

IV. FINDING A BOOK BY ITS CALL NUMBER

Questions 33-38.

DIRECTIONS: The Library of Congress classification system call numbers shown below are arranged in order, just as the books bearing those call numbers would be

8

arranged on the shelves. To show where other call numbers would be located, select the letter of the CORRECT ANSWER.

A.	B.	C.	D.	E.	F.	G.	H.	I.	J.	K.
PS	PS	PS	PS	PS	PS	PS	PS	PS	PS	PS
201	201	208	351	351	3513	3515	3515.3	3526	3526.17	3526.37
.L67	.M44	.B87	.D7	.D77	.A2	.D72	A66	.N21	P2	A10
1961		1944								

L.	M.	N.
PS	PS	PT
3526.37	3526.37	1
C20	C37	.R2

33. A book with the call number PS 201 .L67 would be shelved

A. Before A B. Between A & B C. Between B & C
D. Between C & D E. Between D & E

34. A book with the call number PS 208 .B87 1944a would be shelved

A. Between A & B B. Between C & D C. Between B & C
D. Between C & D E. Between D & E

35. A book with the call number PS 351 D8 would be shelved

A. Between C & D B. Between D & E C. Between E & F
D. Between F & G E. Between G & H

36. A book with the call number PS 3526.3 M53 would be shelved

A. Between L & M B. Between J & K C. Between K & L
D. Between M & 0 E. Between 0 & P

37. A book with the call number PS 3526.37 C205 would be shelved

A. Between L & M B. Between N & 0 C. Between M & N
D. Between 0 & P E. Between P & Q

38. A book with the call number PS 3526.37 C3 would be shelved

A. Between M & N B. Between L & M C. Between N & 0
D. Between 0 & P E. Between P & Q

9

V. General

Questions 39-40.

DIRECTIONS: Each question or incomplete statement is followed by several suggested answers or completions. Select the one that BEST answers the question or completes the statement. *PRINT THE LETTER OF THE CORRECT ANSWER IN TEE SPACE AT THE RIGHT.*

39.   When it is finished (in 610 volumes), the _____ will be the MOST monumental national   39._____
bibliography in the world.

   A.   UNION LIST OF SERIALS IN LIBRARIES OF THE UNITED STATES AND CAN-
        ADA
   B.   UNITED STATES CATALOG
   C.   READERS' GUIDE TO PERIODICAL LITERATURE
   D.   NATIONAL UNION CATALOG

40.   For those who wish to investigate the publishing companies and the people who control   40._____
them, to locate the date a company was founded, who owned it, when it changed hands,
what firm succeeded it, and other information of a similar nature, the periodical _____ is
clearly invaluable.

   A.   PUBLISHERS' TRADE LIST ANNUAL (PTLA)
   B.   CUMULATIVE BOOK INDEX
   C.   AMERICAN BOOKTRADE DIRECTORY
   D.   PUBLISHERS WEEKLY

KEY (CORRECT ANSWERS)

1. I
2. B
3. E
4. C
5. D
6. G
7. H
8. J
9. A
10. C - The first word of the title which is not an article.
11. E - Every book in the library is listed in the card catalog under the author's name. (Warning: The "author" may be a society, a university, or some other institution.)
12. C - A title is alphabetized word-by-word; therefore, "New" comes before "Newsweek," "New York" before "New Yorker."
13. B - The United Nations, not an individual, is the author of this work.
14. T 16. Q 18. D 20. J 22. E 24. A 26. B 28. C 30. F 32. A
15. 0 17. M 19. N 21. K 23. R 25. P/H 27. C 29. D 31. B
33. A - When two call numbers are identical except that one has a year or some other figure added at its end, the shorter call numbers comes first.
34. B
35. C - The numbers which follow a. are regarded as decimals; therefore, .D77 precedes .D8.
36. B - 3526.3 precedes 3526.37
37. A - .C20 precedes .C205
38. B - .C3 precedes .C37 (Read the call number line-by-line, and put a J before a P, before a PB, etc. Put a lower number before a greater one.)
39. D
40. D

ANSWER SHEET

TEST NO. _____ PART _____ TITLE OF POSITION _____

PLACE OF EXAMINATION _____ DATE _____

(CITY OR TOWN)   (STATE)

RATING

USE THE SPECIAL PENCIL.   MAKE GLOSSY BLACK MARKS.

Make only ONE mark for each answer.   Additional and stray marks may be counted as mistakes.   In making corrections, erase errors COMPLETELY.

ANSWER SHEET

TEST NO. _____ PART _____ TITLE OF POSITION _____

PLACE OF EXAMINATION _____

(CITY OR TOWN)   (STATE)   DATE _____

RATING

USE THE SPECIAL PENCIL.   MAKE GLOSSY BLACK MARKS.

Make only ONE mark for each answer.   Additional and stray marks may be counted as mistakes.   In making corrections, erase errors COMPLETELY.